Pregnant
AND
C·H·I·C

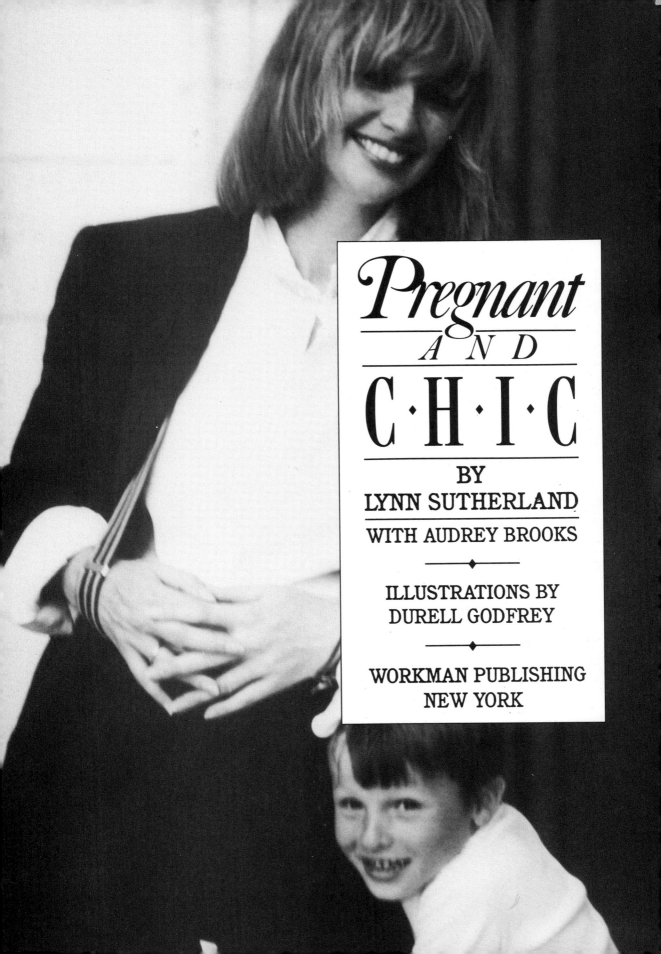

Pregnant
AND
C·H·I·C

BY
LYNN SUTHERLAND

WITH AUDREY BROOKS

◆

ILLUSTRATIONS BY
DURELL GODFREY

◆

WORKMAN PUBLISHING
NEW YORK

To all new mothers,
and to my family and friends.

———◆———

Library of Congress Cataloging-in-Publication Data

Sutherland, Lynn.
Pregnant and chic.

1. Maternity clothes. I. Brooks, Audrey. II. Title.
TT547.S88 1988   646'.34   86-40642
ISBN 0-89480-302-6 (pbk.)

Photographs on pages 34, 58, 76, and 83 by Laurence Le Guay;
photographs on pages 94 and 97 by Ariel Skelly;
all other photographs by Jean-Louis David.

Workman Publishing Company, Inc.
708 Broadway
New York, NY 10003

Printed in the United States of America

First printing April 1989
10 9 8 7 6 5 4 3 2 1

Acknowledgments

To Durell Godfrey I owe boundless thanks for contributing not only her artistic talent and professionalism, but also many wonderful ideas and lots of cheerful encouragement. She was generous beyond the call of duty and a delight to work with.

I'm grateful to Peter and Carolan Workman and to Sally Kovalchick for their enthusiasm and valuable suggestions. A special thanks goes to Carol McKeown for her many hours spent on this book, and to Susan Aronson Stirling, Barbara Scott-Goodman, and the rest of the hardworking staff at Workman Publishing Company.

Many thanks to Alice Martell for her encouragement and guidance; to Audrey Brooks for all her efforts; to Shelley Pentz and Whitney Hess for being such great helpers; and to Ariel Skelly, Jean-Louis David, and Laurence Le Guay for their photography.

Thanks also to Eileen Ford for her encouragement and care and to Catherine Sabino for her support and advice.

Finally, thank you to the interested participants in my interviews and research, and to my friends and family. I owe a great deal of gratitude to the many people I have worked with over the years for their constant inspiration and joy.

Foreword

As I was walking down the street the other day, I spotted a woman who stood out in the crowd. Her hair was glossy and beautifully cut. Her clothes were chic. She looked terrific. And, taking an educated guess, I'd say she was about seven months pregnant.

Pregnancy is no longer the obstacle to looking great that women—and the garment industry—once assumed it was. We have rebelled against the cutesy pastel-print dresses and bows that used to be the uniform of pregnancy, preferring to maintain our dignity and sense of style. Many of us are working straight through our pregnancies, so keeping up a professional image has become a necessity. But being pregnant and chic is more than a survival tactic—it's a way of expressing the confidence, happiness, energy, and spirit your new condition inspires. You can be as fashionable, businesslike, and feminine as ever if you learn some creative ways to adapt your style to your rapidly changing body.

Dressing with style while your waist goes from 26 to 40 inches and back in less than a year is quite a challenge, but it's also fun. And looking wonderful through it all doesn't mean spending a huge amount of money on new clothes. If you have an inventive turn of mind, or can hook into one, you can be chic on a shoestring. This book will help you do it.

My message throughout is to relax, have fun, and enjoy how you look during this exciting time. Experiment and take pride in your creativity. Of course, not every idea I propose will be right for every woman. Our sheer diversity of size, shape, and taste makes that impossible. But you will learn some important fashion principles and then be able to pick and choose among my tips—borrowing, altering, refining—until you find comfortable looks that make you feel good about yourself. What I hope to inspire in *every* reader is a spirit of confidence in her own unique image.

In addition to my personal discoveries, *Pregnant and Chic* offers advice from other new mothers—businesswomen, models, homemakers, and others whom I interviewed and surveyed. Their candid comments about what worked and what didn't will give you insight into your own situation and let you know you're not alone.

Pregnancy is a very special time—one to be treasured and remembered. A time when you feel terrific and want to look great. There's no reason to deny yourself that pleasure, so start shaping your new pregnancy wardrobe now!

—Lynn Sutherland

Contents

INTRODUCTION

The Birth of a Book

This book comes out of a wide range of experiences, going back to my days as a kid in Australia. I was fascinated by fashion from an early age. When I was eight, I inherited my grandmother's turn-of-the-century sewing machine, and before long I had the best-dressed dolls in town. As I grew older, I started turning out clothes for myself. My friend Jennifer and I would spend hours sitting on my parents' veranda sewing new outfits to wear to the beach. Floral Bermuda shorts were our biggest hit.

While still a teenager, I became a fashion model. I first modeled in Sydney, then in Paris and Milan, and eventually with Ford models in New York. Looking back, it seems a miracle that it happened at all. But I am certain that understanding the construction of clothes helped.

My passion for clothes and style made working as a model all the more interesting. I had an incredible opportunity to see the fashion industry close up—from the cutting rooms of designers like Kenzo and Azzedine Alaïa to the editorial offices of Diana Vreeland of American *Vogue.* I worked with the editorial staff of French *Elle* and *Vogue Beauté* and gained hands-on experience with top fashion stylists, makeup artists, and photographers. It was an education I couldn't have gotten any other way.

Through it all, I found my own style emerging. It was a natural outgrowth of the job. After spending all day being remade in a designer's image, I wanted nothing more than to go home and get into some clothes that felt like me—not a designer's fantasy of me. As a model, I was showing the best clothes in the world. But that didn't necessarily mean I wanted to wear them all the time.

What I've learned over the years is, day to day it's far more satisfying to express my own personal style. On a practical level, that means being very selective about what I buy. It means not buying a skirt, blouse, shoes, hat, and jacket all from one designer. Or, if I do, not wearing them all at the same time. It means having the confidence to be a little unorthodox. Because it's these marks of individualism that become your fashion signature.

My personal style tends toward the eclectic—probably a result of my travels. My work for *Vogue, Harper's Bazaar, Glamour,* and *Mademoiselle,* as well as for European, Japanese, and Australian magazines, took me on trips all over the world. Wherever I was on location—Africa, New Guinea, Polynesia—I bought what was for sale at the local markets and mixed it with the things I already owned from the U.S., France, Germany, and Italy. The result is a unique look shaped by the know-how I've picked up over 15 years of modeling.

Pregnant and Panicked

This fashion know-how was given the supreme test one evening in a hotel in Milan. It was a few months after my marriage and I was pregnant. Although I was overjoyed, I had no idea what I was going to do when the clothes in my bag no longer fit. Suddenly—or so it seemed to me—the zipper on my favorite pair of pants simply refused to budge. We were scheduled to meet friends for dinner in half an hour. I panicked. What was I going to wear? Clearly, it was time to get creative.

As I hung my pants back up in the closet, my eyes came to rest on my husband's suit. What did I have to lose? I started with the trousers. I snagged some suspenders, attached them, and took a look in the mirror. Still too roomy. I grabbed a belt, threaded it through the loops, and buckled it, ruffling the extra fabric into a kind of paper-bag waist.

Then I looked down. The hems were dragging on the floor. Cutting them was obviously out of the question, so I pulled

This stylish solution to the maternity-swimwear blues is just one of my fashion brainstorms. Instructions are given in Chapter 6.

my socks up over the bottoms of the pant legs, folding the fabric as you would to stick your pants into a pair of boots. Then I bloused the fabric a bit, jogging-pant style.

Next I had to figure out what to wear on top. I eyed his shirts and tried one on. I turned up the collar and piled on some necklaces and bracelets. Should I go for broke and wear the jacket, too? I put it on and rolled the sleeve of the jacket to midforearm, pushing it up to just above my elbow. I stuck a lacy handkerchief in the pocket and sauntered into the next room, where my husband was waiting. What did he think? He applauded.

Not only was my husband's wardrobe

free for the wearing, but it also offered a wonderful set of uniforms. After all, suits are an internationally respected mode of dressing. I could go just about anywhere dressed this way. I began to experiment with different moods. (You'll see some of the possibilities in Chapter 3.)

Developing a Personal Style

Naturally, I didn't confine myself to men's clothes. Once I started exploring, I found all kinds of chic and inexpensive alternatives to maternity shops and department stores. These included five-and-dime stores, import shops, sporting-goods emporiums, and antique-clothing and secondhand shops. It's more fun to find unusual clothing and put it together in your own way, expressing your own style, than to buy straight off the rack. Because each piece cost so little, I could buy more than I would have at a boutique or department store, so I had more options and changes within the same budget.

Another thing I did as my pregnancy progressed—shades of my girlhood—was to take up sewing again. Since my leisure time was limited, I made only garments that were quick and easy—anyone who can thread a needle can make these pieces. A favorite was an elastic-topped dress that became one of my maternity staples. I must have had at least five of them in different fabrics. They went everywhere—from the beach to gala parties—and proved perfect for nursing, too.

In addition to the clothes I borrowed from my husband, the clothes I bought, and the clothes I sewed, I made good use of the clothes I already had. Nothing was packed away until I had exhausted its maternity possibilities. Waistbands were widened and buttons moved. Blouses with pretty collars worked beautifully under big vests and sweaters, jackets and jumpers. Tube skirts and anything knit grew along with my pregnant body. I was amazed at the clothes I could continue to wear if I took time to devise new and unexpected ways to adapt them.

Spreading the News

Throughout my pregnancy, I was constantly stopped by people on the street who wanted to know where I "bought" my clothes. French *Elle, Parents,* and Australian *Vogue* magazines liked my approach to style so much that they photographed me in my sixth and ninth months and featured my ideas in their pages. I realized I had stumbled onto a good thing. Pregnant women were ready for a change and could benefit from my ideas. I decided to write this book.

Before I started, I wanted to arm myself with some hard facts. I felt it was important to find out how other women managed, or didn't, and precisely what they felt was missing when it came to maternity clothes. So I created some questionnaires and sent them out to several hundred women internationally. I also did a lot of talking to women I felt had made it through their pregnancies with enviable style: models, designers, housewives, businesswomen, journalists, and hairdressers. The tips and tricks I gathered from all these women are an important part of the book. Use it as your springboard to creating a new plan for personal style.

CHAPTER 1

A Guide to the Basics

Many of the tricks and tips in the pages that follow came about through pregnant-and-panicky "What do I do now?" situations. What do I wear to the office, a fancy party, a backyard barbecue, on the tennis court? Each idea is different, designed to rise to a particular occasion, but all of them are based on a few simple principles. Once you learn these basics, you'll understand not only why my ideas worked, but how to create your own special, smashing looks.

The Comfort Factor

The place to begin is with how you feel. During pregnancy, style is nice but comfort is an absolute necessity. Let's not mince words: Pregnancy can be downright uncomfortable. So the clothing you choose should be as comfortable—and comforting—as possible. My advice is, if it doesn't feel good, don't wear it.

Comfort comes as much from the con-struction of clothes as from their fabrics. A piece of clothing has to get high marks in both areas before I'll consider putting it in my closet.

How do you buy comfortable clothes? You have to be aware—at the point of purchase—of how the garment is made as well as how it feels. Look at how a garment is shaped. Blousy shirts, raglan-sleeved sweaters, gathered skirts, and pleated pants all look great and give you room to move and grow. Give the clothes you're considering a trial run. Sit, bend, stretch, and walk in them before you dig into your wallet. As time goes on, you'll be glad that you did.

I learned a lot about comfort from the designer Kenzo, whom I often had the pleasure to work with when I lived in Paris. Kenzo's clothes move with you. They don't bind or restrict. Step into any of his designs and you'll see what I mean. I have a friend who wore Kenzo dresses throughout her whole pregnancy for exactly that reason.

Remember, when you're pregnant you're naturally more self-conscious, constantly trying to get used to a new body. You don't need the added burden of pants that pull, seams that strain, or buttons that don't quite button. If you can put on your clothes and truly forget about them, you'll be able to concentrate on being yourself, radiating confidence in your new look.

The other half of the comfort equation is fabric. What your clothing is made of is important during pregnancy for two reasons. First, pregnancy raises your body temperature. So if you're draped in weighty or stifling fabrics, you're going to feel uncomfortable or unhappy. Second, your body has assumed a new contour. This new shape demands fabrics that drape well. Nothing's worse than clothing that reaches the widest part of your belly and balloons outward from there. So avoid stiff, bulky, or rigid fabrics.

The weight of a fabric is also important to consider. There are six critical fashion months in a pregnancy, and they span at least two seasons. What makes the most sense to me is not to limit your choice of clothing to season-specific fabrics. Instead choose transitional pieces in the first place. Cottons. Light wools. Knits. And then layer them as need be. (The look of layering patterns, fabrics, and colors for pregnancy is one I love.)

If you're pregnant in the summer, it's essential to steer clear of fibers that don't allow your skin to breathe and perspiration to evaporate. Cotton is king here, but pure cotton can shrink and wrinkle. If you're looking for easy care, opt for blends that contain cotton. A blend of at least half natural fiber and half synthetic is best.

The feel of a fabric can be a source of immense pleasure. The right ones can do wonders for your skin and psyche. Silk and cashmere, cozy cotton knits, velvety soft wools, fleecy sweatshirts, matte jerseys, and gentle flannels all feel wonderful, especially when you're pregnant.

Every woman has a preference for certain fabrics. Elaine Learson, the New York editor for *Vogue Homme* and fashion consultant for Bijan, loves leather. At the beginning of her pregnancy, her uniform consisted of a riding jacket worn over a leather skirt, topped off with a fur fling around her neck. (Anything's possible, if you've got the spirit to see it through.) As her pregnancy progressed, Elaine switched into her husband's cashmere sweaters—another tactile treat—over plain black pants. Marsha Stein, a professor of home economics in Connecticut, loved wearing matte jersey when she was pregnant. And because Marsha sews, she was able to use it in everything from suits to gowns. Experiment to find the fabrics you really like. Pregnancy is the perfect time to indulge yourself.

Considering Color

Color has an incredible influence on you and the people around you. It affects your outlook as well as your energy level. Some colors even create physiological responses. For instance, hot colors like magenta, red, and orange can actually make the heart beat faster. Cool ones like green and blue create a relaxing and quieting response. But most responses to color are subjective. The most important thing is to wear those colors that make you feel good, positive, and strong.

To show you how subjective color preferences can be, take black. Many people consider black a downbeat, depressing

Accessories Make a Difference

If you've followed my advice and invested in some flattering, comfortable, solid-colored clothes, you can change the looks just by switching accessories. Say you're starting with navy. One day, you'll do all the accessories in taxicab yellow. The next you'll do only white. Another day, navy and white polka dots. Or red. Or lime green. Or cinnamon. Mix prints and plaids. Each color and type of accessory can dramatically change the mood of the outfit. Hats, socks, gloves, shoes, watches, and bags are all part of the accessory mix. And used with balance and proportion, they're all pure magic. (For some specific accessorizing tips, see Chapter 8.)

color—especially for a pregnant woman. I think it's provocative. One of the sexiest outfits I wore was not particularly revealing, but there was something about the look that always elicited a positive response and made me feel good. It started with a plain black jersey chemise, which I bought one size larger than usual. Over that I wore a black leather blouson jacket that came just under my tummy. I wound gold necklaces around the collar, then flipped it up to make my neck look less scrawny. Dark stockings, heels, and sometimes my raccoon fling finished the outfit. The combination never failed to turn heads. So much for the negative associations with black.

Some of us never really take the time to assess which colors look best. If that's the case for you, seeing a color analyst might help. During a typical session, the analyst will hold up a variety of different colors to your face and help you decide which ones complement you best. A computer consultant who had her colors done right before she became pregnant reports: "The colors the analyst chose for me were quite a bit brighter than the neutrals I usually wore. But I did go out and buy clothes in many of the recommended colors. The compliments I got amazed me. People were convinced I'd done something to myself, but they couldn't figure out what. Some thought I'd dyed my hair. Others thought I was wearing more makeup."

The best way to use color analysis is to temper it with personal discernment. Resist taking the analyst's advice as dogma. Decide for yourself what changes you want to make. And don't feel you have to go out and buy all new clothes. Sometimes a neck scarf in a fabulous new shade is enough.

To save money, you can duplicate the analysis at home. We all do it on a small scale when we hold up a blouse, dress, or sweater to our face in the store mirror. Gather up a bunch of your clothes in a variety of colors. Sit in front of a well-lit mirror and experiment. You'll notice that some colors make your skin look rosier, your eyes brighter, and your hair shinier. Keep these in mind when you shop.

As your waist expands, you can use certain colors to give yourself a more streamlined appearance. While bright and light colors are likely to make you look shorter and heavier, darker colors are slimming. But you don't always have to dress in the darkest colors. Sticking to toned-down versions of your favorite brighter

Create a Slimmer Silhouette

One valuable hint about using color is to carry the same tone from head to toe. This creates a long vertical line, making you look tall and slim. While the effect at left is good—using a long open jacket and dark tie as vertical accents—the one at right is better because the line of color doesn't break at the knee.

A GOOD LOOK BUT CHOPPY

LONGER AND LEANER— LEGS + SHOES + SKIRT ARE THE SAME DARK TONES

colors does the job. Try cranberry or maroon rather than red, navy instead of bright blue, rust in lieu of popsicle orange. Wear a light-colored top, but lengthen your line by making skirt, stockings, and shoes the same dark tone. If you love brights, use them in accessories.

In choosing multicolored fabrics, don't avoid bold patterns, but do choose subtle shades. As always, vertical stripes will make you look taller, and horizontal ones will only emphasize your girth. Get in the habit of using vertical lines whenever possible to distract people from glaring at your middle. Add a necktie, use details like pleats and plackets, or create a long vertical line with a wrap.

Play Up Your Best Parts

Maternity clothes are notorious for covering up your whole body rather than accentuating any part of it. But deciding which parts of your body to play up and which to play down is critical—especially when you're pregnant. Every look needs a focus, a point of view. While you probably wouldn't choose to accentuate your waist at this time, you no doubt have other assets worth emphasizing.

Perhaps your legs are your strong point. Pregnancy won't change that. Make the most of them by being certain your hems hit the most flattering place on your legs. For most women the target spot is just above the curve of their calves. And there are lots of other ways to spotlight your legs. You may want to wear knit pants with big tops, close-to-the-body tube skirts, skirts or suits with slits, patterned hose, or great socks. One model I know wore an elastic-waisted leather miniskirt constantly during her pregnancy. A French painter made a uniform out of tights, tube skirts, and long pullovers. Another model skipped the skirt, wearing just tights and pullover for a great leg show.

Arms, like legs, are hardly affected by pregnancy and are wonderful to highlight. Details like spaghetti straps, cap sleeves, halters, and cutouts are all capable of creating some allure—big belly and all.

If you have a long, graceful neck, draw attention to it with a flattering neckline, an open-necked blouse, or a V-neck. Other attention-getting tactics include wearing an interesting necklace or drop earrings and putting your hair up. Learn to wear turtlenecks pulled up high—not folded down—to give your neck a longer line.

A great back remains a great back—no matter what changes are occurring in front. When she was four months pregnant, model Yasmine bought a backless dress by designer Azzedine Alaïa in three different colors. Eight months after giving birth to her daughter she wears the dress just as much, though now she cinches the waist with a belt. Backless dresses are relatively easy to find. But you really don't have to invest a cent to bare your back. Take any of your V-neck T-shirts and sweaters, turn them around, and they become instant back-barers. Pin a brooch at the tip of the V for even more emphasis. When you're shopping, keep an eye out for the full range of back-view details: racing backs, crisscrossed straps, cut-in sleeves, and halters.

Of course, no discussion about looking sexy would be complete without talking about the bust. You don't need me to tell you a beautiful bustline is worth showing off. Or that hormonal changes during pregnancy have a tendency to create bustlines and cleavage where none existed before. Should you play them up? Absolutely. Think of wearing sheer white blouses over lacy camisoles, unbuttoned just enough to allow some lace to peek out. Or contrast the masculinity of a man's white dinner jacket ('50s vintage) with the femininity of a black lace camisole. The options are endless. Pick one and make the most of it.

A Sense of Proportion

Most of us know our bodies fairly well. We know which styles, shapes, silhouettes, and necklines look best. But when our bellies start growing, everything is suddenly thrown out of proportion. Not to worry. Two pregnancies gave me plenty of time to figure it all out.

The key is maintaining balance. Adding width at the shoulders, cinching fabric in at the hips, and emphasizing vertical lines all help create a more pulled-together, in-control appearance. It's also important, with such a large middle, that whatever you wear on your extremities—neck, head, wrists, ankles—be very close to your body. Hats should be small, with no oversized brims. Sleeves ought to be caught at the wrist. And pants should be brought tight to the ankle.

Here are a few tricks that will help you keep everything under control. You'll see them used repeatedly throughout the book.

SHOULDER PADS

At the top of my list of fashion godsends are shoulder pads. Try on a pair and see what an incredible difference they make. Instantly, your proportion looks more balanced. When your lower half is bulkier than your upper half, they help to compensate. Shoulder pads also allow clothes to hang better. You look altogether less droopy!

Lucky for us, there are plenty of options available at just about every department, discount, notion, or sewing store. So

you can easily add a bolder shoulder to virtually any sweater, top, dress, jacket, or coat. You'll see that there are a variety of

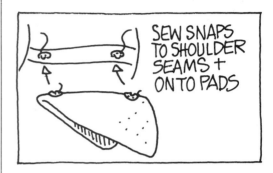

shapes targeted to different sleeve styles—raglan, set-in, dropped shoulder—and various fabric weights. It's best to try them on with the garment to make sure you choose the right ones. If the fabric is thick enough, you may be able to pin the pad on or tuck it under your bra strap. Tucking it under your strap has the added advantage

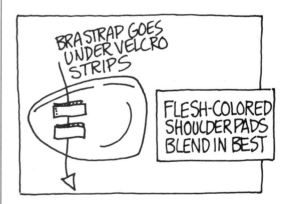

of allowing you to move the pad around easily for proper placement. For thinner fabrics, it may be best to sew the pad on. Or you can try one of those undershirts with shoulder pads built right in. Some pads are sold with strips of Velcro on them so you can use them interchangeably in a number of garments. One photographic stylist found that if the pad had Velcro attached, it stayed put in sweaters without having to sew on the corresponding piece of Velcro. The newest pads are made of bare foam rubber and need no pins, snaps, or Velcro. Their shape and texture keep them in place.

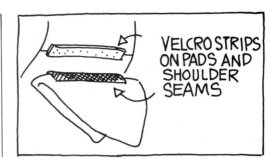

VELCRO STRIPS ON PADS AND SHOULDER SEAMS

Add Shoulder Pads for Balance

When you're pregnant your widest area moves from chest or hips to tummy. Shoulder pads add width to help minimize the bulkiness below. Your proportion is instantly improved. Try them in everything—even T-shirts.

POOH

POW!

SHOULDER PADS AND ROLLED SLEEVES CAN MAKE THE DIFFERENCE

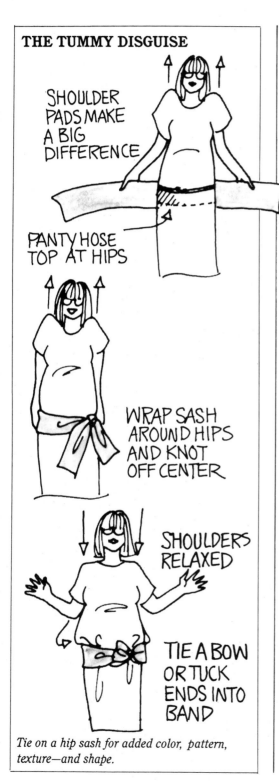

THE TUMMY DISGUISE

SHOULDER PADS MAKE A BIG DIFFERENCE

PANTY HOSE TOP AT HIPS

WRAP SASH AROUND HIPS AND KNOT OFF CENTER

SHOULDERS RELAXED

TIE A BOW OR TUCK ENDS INTO BAND

Tie on a hip sash for added color, pattern, texture—and shape.

THE HIP SASH

Second only to shoulder pads for streamlining pregnant proportions is the hip sash. Ironic though it may sound, sashing the hips actually makes them look smaller. You can sash dresses, tunics, caftans, T-shirts, men's shirts, and any garment that extends beyond your hips. If you're worried about your derriere becoming a focal point, you needn't. With the technique I recommend, it really doesn't. Your whole silhouette will appear slimmer, simply because there's less fabric floating indiscriminately around your body.

To tie a sash you need a length of fabric long enough to go around your hips, plus 12 to 18 inches for tying a bow. (You can get away with less if you opt to just knot the sash or pin it closed.) As for width, 4 inches, more or less, is fine. The sash can be made of just about any material. Wool jersey is a favorite of mine. I've also used wide grosgrain ribbon, silk scarves, silk ties, jute, and gauze. If you use a length of fabric that tends to fray, finish the edges by turning ¼ inch under and topstitching.

First, hunch your shoulders toward your ears and wrap the sash around you as you would a towel. (See illustration.) Make a knot over one hip. Release your shoulders and let the garment blouse over your belly. Tie a bow or tuck the ends behind the sash.

One obstacle to sash satisfaction is that the sash often doesn't stay in place on the garment. A solution I suggest is to cut off the top of a large pair of panty hose and use it as an "undersash." The hose grabs the garment securely—but not uncomfortably—and keeps the decorative sash on top from moving. Friends have said that as they neared the end of their pregnancies they actually liked the girdling feeling of the hose. And I did, too.

A Dozen Indispensables

There is a short but all-important list of clothing items without which I could never have survived two pregnancies in comfort and style. You'll see these crop up over and over on the following pages, most of them going from office to party to weekend-at-home with graceful ease. Since we're talking basics here, I offer you a dozen indispensables—simple, inexpensive items that will be the backbone of your pregnancy wardrobe.

- Boxer shorts, to use as shorts or even as underwear.

- T-shirts of all colors, in large sizes.

- White cotton men's dress shirts—the kind many men wear to work every day. With collars up, sleeves rolled, and pads added, they put punch into all manner of layered looks.

- Jogging or men's pajama pants, with drawstring or elasticized waists.

- Leggings—thick tights without feet that serve as pants under long sweaters and tunics.

- A plain-colored, full-cut dress that can be belted or not and accessorized to give it dozens of different looks.

- A cotton kimono, to be used as a dress, a robe, a cover-up . . . you'll see.

- A dark, unconstructed jacket in light wool or linen, for adding style and a longer line, as well as warmth.

- Several *pareos*—lengths of colorful fabric used for wrapping around you to become skirts, halter tops, dresses, or swimsuit cover-ups.

- Men's bikini underwear—in cotton, without the pocket. As I'll prove later, these are wonderful as maternity underwear and as part of an ingenious swimsuit.

- A good pair of lightweight aerobic shoes, in black or white.

- A pair of low black pumps.

TAMING SLEEVES AND TROUSER HEMS

One technique I devised in the first raid on my husband's closet (described in the Introduction) helps to promote the neat-extremities look. It is a way of folding the sleeves of a shirt and jacket. Either put them on and roll both sleeves together, or turn the jacket sleeve back once or twice, roll the shirtsleeve, and tuck the rolled jacket into the rolled shirtsleeve. Then push everything up toward your elbow, as illustrated.

Another trick is helpful when you want to shorten a pant leg but can't trim and hem to get the right length (that is, when

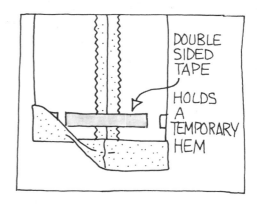

your husband would rather not have *his* pants shortened). Put the pants on and pin the legs up to the desired length. Take them off and lightly steam (too heavy and you'll make a permanent crease) the tem-

The Sleeve Trick

It may seem simple to roll up your sleeves, but there *are* chic ways to do it—and sloppy ways to avoid. The method illustrated here guarantees a put-together look and is especially helpful when you're wearing menswear. Along with shoulder pads, it adds shape and style while creating a better fit.

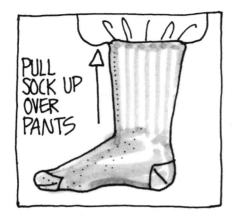

PULL SOCK UP OVER PANTS

EVENLY SCRUNCH SOCK DOWN TO ANKLE

MAKES A "JOGGING" EFFECT

porary hem. Then use double-sided tape, as shown, to hold the hem in place.

A third trick is to gather pant legs into your socks. With soft fabrics, you can create a jogging-style bottom by pulling the sock up over the pant leg and then scrunching it down to your ankle. (This is what I did in the photo opposite.) With stiffer fabrics, make one deep, forward fold on each side of your ankle and hold the pleats with your socks. Blouse the pant leg a bit and scrunch the sock down.

Read on to discover how to put all these basics to work for you. You'll be amazed at what a big difference a few small changes can make. Now you're thinking chic!

Stepping out in menswear styled to flatter the pregnant figure.

CHAPTER 2

Strategy for the Early Months

First your pregnancy test comes back positive. Then, sometimes, you have morning sickness. But you don't *really* believe you're pregnant until one day the skirt that always fit so well doesn't fit at all. And instead of feeling upset because a few pounds have sneaked up on you, you feel overjoyed. Finally there's absolute proof. You are really pregnant!

Most women begin losing their waists sometime during the second or third month of pregnancy. If it's your second pregnancy, it might even be sooner. Thus begins a transitional period lasting one or two months, when you are too small for the voluminous clothes you'll need later and too big for many of your regular clothes. At this point, it's very hard to imagine how much your body will ultimately change. One woman I know bought a few skirts one size larger when she was about three months along. She thought that since the waists were quite roomy they'd last several months. She wasn't even close. In just a couple of weeks she had to retire them to the back of her closet.

It's best not to invest in any new clothes now. Instead, try to work with what you already have on hand. Once you learn to think creatively, you'll be amazed at the possibilities. Waistbands can be extended, shirts worn over skirts instead of tucked in, dresses left unbelted.

Knits, roomy sweaters, and any garments with elastic waistbands are particularly useful during this transitional time—as well as later, when you're getting back into shape after the birth (much more on that in Chapter 10). In fact, if you simply can't resist the urge to buy, put your money in knits. One fashion magazine editor splurged on a knit tunic and pull-on pants by Sonia Rykiel at the beginning of her pregnancy. She wore the outfit until the last couple of months, then began wearing it again after the baby was born. "It was expensive, but it more than paid for itself both in comfort and the amount of wear I got out of it."

As time goes on, you may want to take a look at the newest skirts and pants in the maternity shops. Some of the innovative new designs are worth your attention.

Bridging the Waistband Gap

With all of today's roomy sweaters and vests, long jackets, and big pullovers—it's fairly easy to make your tops serve well into your pregnancy. Dresses, skirts, and pants tend to be less forgiving, but there are ways to stretch their usefulness, too.

If you own a dress with a belt but no defined waist, remove the belt or simply sash the dress lower on the hip and add shoulder pads to balance out the inches at the waist. The lives of both skirts and pants can be extended quite easily—even the straightest, most tailored skirts. When you're first beginning to show, use pins to create some breathing room. Diaper pins are safest. Leave the zipper open as much as you need for comfort and cover the gap with longer tops or jackets—no more tucked-in tops! When a pin's width doesn't do the job, it's time to change techniques.

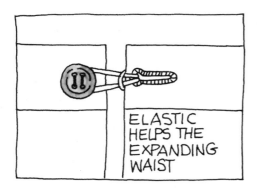

ELASTIC HELPS THE EXPANDING WAIST

The simplest method of expansion I've come across is to hook a rubber band to the button hole and lasso the button with the other end. The great thing about rubber bands is that they stretch with you as you grow but don't harm fabric in any way. You can attach them to leather or suede without worrying about causing permanent damage. With their help, you can wear many of your skirts and pants for weeks to come.

Another way to extend the waistband is to sew a three-inch piece of elastic to one side of the opening. Then pin the elastic to the other side. If you're handy—or know a

Sew in a Maternity Panel

To expand a skirt permanently, buy a stretch panel at a fabric store. Trace around the panel with chalk, cut out the area ¾ inch inside the mark, and sew the panel on top, covering the raw edge. The panel will stretch with you, allowing the skirt to fall straight below it.

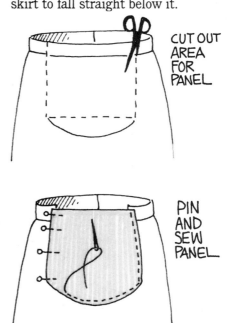

CUT OUT AREA FOR PANEL

PIN AND SEW PANEL

good seamstress—you can create a more permanent attachment by removing the waistbands of favorite skirts or pants, opening up the side seams, and connecting the gaps with elastic. The waistband can be reattached after pregnancy. This way the hem will remain fairly even, although the front will get shorter as you get bigger.

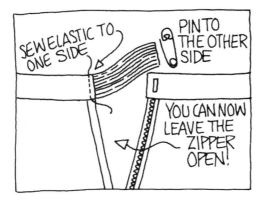

If you have any old suits or skirts you don't mind altering irrevocably, you can add stretch panels to the fronts—look for them at fabric stores and notions departments—thus creating a skirt that will last you comfortably for many months. Lay the panel on your skirt and use tailors' chalk to mark around it. Cut out the area about ¾ inch inside your mark, pin the panel to the outside of the skirt, and sew by hand or machine.

Totally Terrific T-Shirts

One of the best boons for pregnancy from the early months on is the T-shirt. Not the fancy designer kind, but the standard-issue men's T-shirts that come three to a package. They're inexpensive, comfortable, versatile, and—most important—expandable. And, with a little creative play, they can be turned into an unflagging supply of maternity tops for a veritable song.

T-shirts are especially great for pregnant women who fill out in the bust before anywhere else. My friend was like that. She increased two bra sizes in the first three months and couldn't fit into any of her regular tops. T-shirts saved her sanity. She wore T-shirts with jeans, T-shirts with leggings, with pajama or jogging pants, and even T-shirts under suits for work (a look you can get away with only while the T is very crisp).

If you don't think a T-shirt is appropriate for your office, use it as a first layer. Then add a very large and very luxe silk scarf over it, so that most of the T-shirt is covered. Knot the scarf in back bib-style. This allows the scarf lots of show in front and covers up most of the T-shirt. If your office atmosphere is more casual, try large Ts over plain knit dresses. Enlarge the neckline by cutting off the ribbing—let the edge roll back naturally and roll up the sleeves, as shown on page 31. Or wear two at once, cutting the top shirt short and rolling the cuffs to show both colors.

One fashion consultant I talked to has a sensible approach to wearing T-shirts with skirts or pants. She layers them, putting on a small T first, to anchor her shoulder pads firmly in place and create a snug band around her neck. Then she adds a large shirt on top to cover her tummy. (You can cut the small T off under your bust if it won't span your waist.)

Men's T-shirts come in standard colors of white, black, navy, light blue, forest green, and yellow. But exotic colors are popping up more and more frequently. I recently found orange and purple at my local discount store.

T-Shirt Savvy

The simple T-shirt is like a blank canvas, easy to improve on with a little know-how. And especially during the early months, it can help your wardrobe expand as you do! Here, a sampler of ways to add chic on the cheap (don't forget your shoulder pads).

TIE UP SLEEVES OF A V-NECK T-SHIRT — (RIBBON IS FESTIVE)

- Gather the tops of the sleeves up to the shoulder seams and tie them with ribbons threaded through the sleeve and neck openings.

- Pick up rhinestones or little pearls at a craft shop and glue or sew them around the neck and hem.

- Paint the T-shirt with fabric paint. You might write your favorite boys' and girls' names. Your due date. The hospital you'll be using.

CUT AWAY NECK RIBBING AND STITCH

USE AN EXTRA LONG T-SHIRT

TIE AT HIPS AND BLOUSE

- Open side seams about 5 inches, run ribbons through the hem casing, and tie at each hip.

PADS

TWIST AND KNOT EXCESS FABRIC

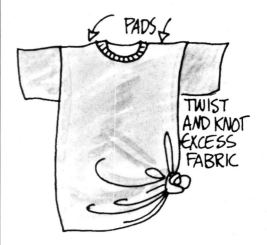

- Pull the bottom of the T so it's tight across your hips. Twist and knot the excess fabric. If there's not enough to knot, secure it with a brooch.

ROLL TOGETHER

TRIM TO MID RIBCAGE

WEAR OVER A WHITE T-SHIRT

- Use two Ts in contrasting colors, say white and black. Cut the black one to rib-cage height and pull it over the white one. Then roll the sleeves up so you see a fold of white on each arm.

WITH A HUGE T-SHIRT YOU CAN SLIT + TIE AT BOTH SIDES

PADS, TOO

TAKE IN EXCESS AT SIDES

WITH PRETTY RIBBON

- Cut five-inch slits up the sides of the T. Knot the two ends together and blouse. Or leave the slits open and add ties at the sides that you can let out gradually as you need room.

ROLL CUFFS TO SHOW COLORS

A CROPPED T-SHIRT OVER A BLACK DRESS-

HEM A T-SHIRT SHORTER + LAYER OVER THE LONGER ONE

RED OVER WHITE OVER BLACK

- Layer one T-shirt (or more) over a plain knit dress. Widen the T-shirt's neckline by cutting, rolling the edge under, and topstitching.

The Art of Fashion Brainstorming

Knit tops and altered waistbands are commonsensical solutions to a changing figure. But now, and throughout your pregnancy, you need to open your mind to more daring innovations. That's what this book is all about. Just taking a few minutes to play with your clothes and accessories can yield numerous new solutions and combinations that may not strike you as you stare blankly into the closet. Look at old favorites in new ways. And don't be afraid to fail. Only you and the mirror will know.

Here are two examples of how my fashion brainstorming paid off.

THE VERSATILE DRESS

While rummaging through my closet one day, I discovered a dress that I had used again and again when I was modeling. It is basically a tube of fabric held up by an elastic casing that sits just above the bust. (See photo on page 26.) The dress had been born out of desperation, really. Being a modest person, I was horrified when fashion editors and photographers regularly asked that I change clothes in public. For a while, I pulled sheets over my head and dressed underneath—which didn't endear me to hairdressers. Or asked someone to hold a blanket around me. Then one day during a photo shoot in a marketplace on the edge of the Sahara, I came up with the tube dress.

I made it in a hurry, using a length of fabric I bought at one of the stalls and the shoelaces off my sneakers instead of elastic. The dress was so roomy I could dress—or undress—inside of it, which is exactly what I did. Later I made the dress out of all kinds of interesting fabrics bought at exotic locations. By the time I stopped modeling I had quite a collection.

Rediscovering these dresses early in my pregnancy triggered further brainstorms. During the first few months, I sashed them at the hip and my belly was hardly noticeable. As the months went on and I grew bigger, I just let the fabric sail over my stomach.

The dress adapts well to a variety of needs. It can be casual or elegant. Worn with a blazer or sweater, it's sporty. Add an evening wrap or shawl and it's dressy. For the summer months, make the dress out of cotton or linen. For winter, use light wool or gabardine, add straps, and wear it with a sweater or blouse underneath. And for evening, use fancy fabric such as velvet or taffeta (see page 79).

THE FINISHED DRESS

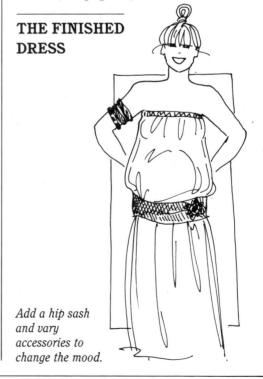

Add a hip sash and vary accessories to change the mood.

The Versatile Dress—Short or Long, Casual or Formal

Here's a dress that can take you from home to the office to a party, depending on the length, fabric, and accessories you choose. It's a cinch to make with a machine in a matter of minutes. By hand, it takes a bit longer. Here's how:

LEAVE A BIT OPEN TO THREAD ELASTIC INTO CASING

- For a knee-length dress, use 36- or 45-inch-wide fabric, depending on your height and how long you want the dress to be. For a long dress, you may need to buy 60-inch fabric. Buy enough to reach three times around your normal waist. You'll also need a package of half-inch elastic, thread, needles, scissors, and pins.

- Fold the fabric in half widthwise, right sides together. Pin and sew a seam down the side opening.

- Turn the top edge down and sew a ¾-inch casing. Wrap a tape measure under your arms, around your back, and above your bust to determine the length of the elastic. Cut the elastic and thread it through the casing. Try the dress on and adjust the elastic to fit snugly. Remove the dress and hand-sew the opening in the casing closed.

- If the selvage looks finished along the bottom, you may not have to hem. If it's ragged, or you want to alter the length, pin and hem.

- Add a hip wrap and other accessories to fit the occasion. *Voilà!*

- To make a matching shawl, hem a 36- or 45-inch square of fabric. To wear, fold it into a triangle and tie it in front or fasten it with a pin. Or you might pull it over one shoulder and tie it on the diagonal. A charming look.

THE DOUBLE PULLOVER

Another creative flash I had in my first few months was a fabulous knit ensemble. One day I was rummaging around in a drawer and came across a huge old V-neck sweater in a charcoal gray. I pulled it on over my head, bypassing my arms completely, and continued to pull it down until the neck became a waist and the body of the sweater became a skirt. The arms hung down, so I tucked them inside-out, like pockets, and rolled up the cuffs so they didn't dangle below the "skirt's" hemline. The effect was fine from the hips down but a little lumpy above. What I needed was a top that reached to the hips. Easy enough. I found

This innovative sweater set offers both comfort and class. Wear it to work or out to dinner on a wintry evening.

THE INSIDE STORY

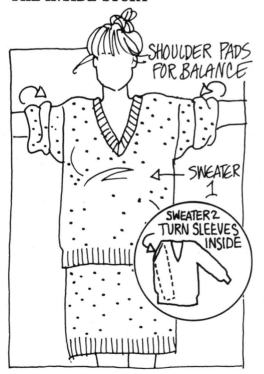

Use one sweater as a skirt, tucking the sleeves inside-out and rolling them up so they don't hang below the hem.

an oversized black sweater and added shoulder pads for a better line across the top. The result was a natty little sweater suit I could wear just about anywhere.

If this look is for you, try a variety of color combinations to find the most flattering. A cherry-red sweater on a black bottom is beautifully classic. Darker colors will give you a longer, leaner line. Any sweater with an extra-large neck opening—a boat neck, for instance—will work as the "skirt." If you don't have any sweaters big enough, check thrift shops or army/navy stores for low-priced ones. For really long sweaters, see tall-men's shops in your area. You'll wear them often throughout your pregnancy, so they're worth the price.

First Stop at the Maternity Shop

For many women, especially those pregnant for the first time, buying bonafide maternity clothes is a rite of passage—like passing your pregnancy test and eating crackers for nausea. Versatility and fashion brainstorming are fun and economical, but there's something about a store-bought maternity outfit that makes your condition seem official. A homemaker and mother of two admits, "I bought my first pair of maternity pants when I was two-and-a-half months pregnant. I didn't really need them, but I got the biggest kick out of wearing them, anyway. Just having them on made me feel more pregnant."

In the last several years there has been a definite trend toward more fashionable maternity wear, aimed at satisfying today's sophisticated mother-to-be. So it does pay to take a look at what's in the shops, as long as you make your choices carefully. One woman who represents a number of maternity-wear manufacturers offers this advice: Take the time to find a store whose merchandise you really like. Check out all the stores in your area and then shop at the one that appeals to you most. Next, find a salesperson who's really interested and enthusiastic and knows the shop's stock. Try to avoid picking up odd pieces here and there. Since maternity wardrobes are usually limited, it's important to buy coordinated pieces that you can mix and match easily. Choose a color scheme early on and stick to it for maximum versatility.

With oversized tops so available in regular departments, maternity tops have become practically obsolete in recent years unless they are part of an ensemble—skirt, pants, and perhaps a jacket. Many true maternity tops are made with a wide band at the bottom, which works like a hip sash to bring the fabric in closer to the body while letting the fabric blouse over it. Some designers have begun using non-maternity details like ribbing to create the same effect in a classier style. What's really new in maternity stores are bottoms. Here's a roundup of the styles that are worth looking for.

THE BOTTOMS TO BUY

One of the biggest developments in maternity clothing in recent years has been the evolution of the maternity panel. The stretch "pouch" was the only alternative for the longest time. But then the market was invaded by maverick designers, many of them new mothers with no formal training who decided there had to be a better way to dress. The results are varied and offer lots of choices.

A radical departure from the pouch is the Obi Kutsurogi, designed by Barbie White of Japanese Weekend. The words mean "comfort sash" in Japanese and the O.K., as it is trademarked, is being used in skirts, pants, shorts—and even underpants (see page 137). Instead of covering the abdomen, the O.K. saddles and supports it from underneath. A wide elastic band begins at the small of the back and then curves lower in the front to just below your tummy. The big benefit, aside from support, is that you don't have to worry about the pant or skirt fitting differently as your size changes. Since it doesn't cover your belly, the garment and its hem aren't affected by your growth. And skirts stay attractively narrow because they begin below your belly.

Skirts and Slacks—
Best Choices from off the Racks

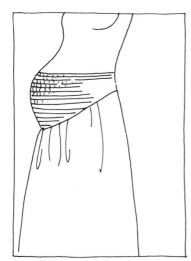

Shirred panel waistline

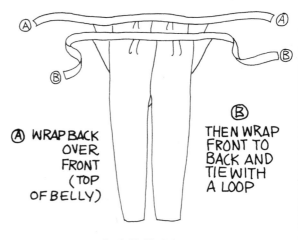

Ⓐ WRAP BACK OVER FRONT (TOP OF BELLY)

Ⓑ THEN WRAP FRONT TO BACK AND TIE WITH A LOOP

Janit Baldwin's wrap pants

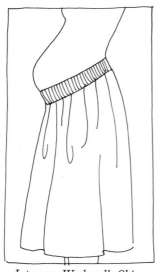

Japanese Weekend's Obi Kutsurogi, or "O.K.," style

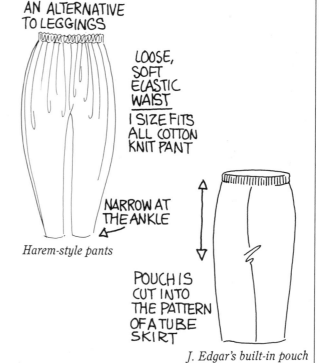

AN ALTERNATIVE TO LEGGINGS

LOOSE, SOFT ELASTIC WAIST

1 SIZE FITS ALL COTTON KNIT PANT

NARROW AT THE ANKLE

Harem-style pants

POUCH IS CUT INTO THE PATTERN OF A TUBE SKIRT

J. Edgar's built-in pouch

Another new solution is the shirred panel designed by Marilyn Stern for Ninth Moon. An advance in both looks and comfort, Ninth Moon's panel could be mistaken for a design element. Once it's on, it hugs the tummy securely but not tightly. Like the O.K., it allows the skirt to begin below the tummy so that it falls gracefully close to the legs.

Some designs manage to avoid the idea of a maternity panel entirely. One comfortable style, sometimes called a harem pant, is cleverly designed and cut so that most of the expansive room is contained in the elasticized back. Like the best new maternity pants, these reflect the realization that most women don't lose all their weight within weeks of giving birth. Because pants like these are not obviously "maternity pants," a woman can feel comfortable wearing them for a long time after the baby is born—making the initial investment much easier to rationalize.

In recent years, a new type of harem pant has become popular among all women—not just pregnant ones. This is a cotton knit pant with a soft elastic waistband that draws in a large volume of fabric. The one-size-fits-all pants stretch easily to fit pregnant tummies and narrow at the ankle for the controlled look you need. Wear them as alternatives to leggings. They are often sold along with large tops (and shoulder pads, of course), hip wraps, and other items to mix and match.

Janit Baldwin's designs are adaptations of traditional Japanese field pants, a wrap style that makes a lot of sense for pregnancy. The slits on each side guarantee breathing room. The back and front wraps allow the pant to fit tighter or more loosely, depending on your size, and can be tied at the sides at full term.

J. Edgar, a California designer, uses elastic waistbands, then cuts the fronts bigger and higher to create a sort of barely discernible pouch. After the baby is born, you can take in the pouch with a simple seam and move the skirt back into your regular wardrobe. The waistband itself is made of "draw-cord elastic," which allows you to adjust the fit from early pregnancy through your largest time and back again.

One style that has been enormously popular—for good reason—has a buttoned and pleated waistband designed to be unbuttoned pleat by pleat as you grow. The big advantage is that you can button it back down to a small size as you get back into shape. Many maternity jeans are similarly designed.

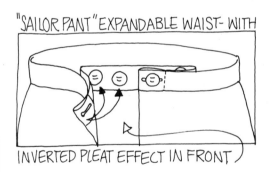

"SAILOR PANT" EXPANDABLE WAIST- WITH INVERTED PLEAT EFFECT IN FRONT

V-shaped elastic inserts are sometimes used on the sides of pants or skirts to allow for flat fronts as well as backs. This is another style that can be worn during and after pregnancy. A nice plus.

Now you've stretched your pre-pregnancy wardrobe and splurged on some maternity-shop staples. Your waist is rapidly expanding and it's time to get more creative. Let the real brainstorming begin!

CHAPTER 3

Great Finds from Unexpected Sources

With the exception of a few pieces, my entire pregnancy wardrobe was made up of what I'll call "alternative" clothes. Perhaps that's why I was stopped on the street so much. What I was wearing looked good and was so different from what most people expected a pregnant woman to wear that they just had to ask where I bought my clothes. When I explained that my suit was really my husband's, or my dress was actually from a thrift shop, they were astonished. Most people just assumed that pregnant women had to shop in maternity stores.

But men's departments, thrift shops, five-and-dime stores, sporting-goods stores, and uniform shops—not your typical sources for the latest and greatest in maternity clothes—are a gold mine of unique looks at irresistible prices.

It does take some looking to ferret out the treasures, though, as well as a sense of how to combine things to best effect. I like to compare this kind of shopping to antiquing: The most amazing things often turn up in the least likely places. Naturally you wouldn't furnish your entire home with furniture that you'd picked up at one neighborhood antique store. Nor would you buy your whole wardrobe at a discount store. But one or two pieces from either place can add a touch of personality and style to home or wardrobe.

There's also the fun and satisfaction of putting an outfit together and the thrill of wearing your own creation—especially when you receive admiring comments.

No question about it. If you want to project an individual style and save money, you have to explore alternative sources for your maternity wardrobe. This chapter will open your eyes to some of the best.

Your Husband's Closet

One of the most convenient places to shop is, of course, your husband's closet. As I mentioned in the Introduction, I discovered the possibilities of my husband's wardrobe out of desperation but soon came to rely on it for good looks, comfort, and versatility. Turning to his closet offers a number of advantages—you can shop at home, the choice is terrific, and the prices are unbeatable. But you should have his permission to search and deploy.

If your husband's physique and your growing figure are not very compatible, borrow from the other men in your life. Fathers, brothers, and grandfathers can be made sympathetic to your cause. And if that's not possible, you can always turn to the men's sections of thrift and secondhand stores.

The biggest objection women have to wearing men's clothes is that they might mask their femininity. And that might be true if you were to wear men's clothes exactly as men do. But you won't. My idea is to adapt men's clothes to a woman's body and point of view. That means rolling sleeves, turning up collars, adding shape with shoulder pads and sashes, and creating femininity with lacy collars and scarves. Making use of color and mixing patterns the way a man wouldn't. Rolling up pant legs so your textured socks show. Piling on pins and bracelets and chains. Running the gamut so people notice style first and clothing gender last.

I was lucky. My husband gave me free rein with his wardrobe. And, just as important, we were close enough in size so that his clothing and my expanding body combined nicely. I wore his summer and winter suits, his sweaters, golf cardigans, and sports jackets. His karate or baseball pants, both designed for comfort and ease of movement, worked beautifully as casual pants teamed with flannel or cotton shirts or sweatshirts. I played around with anything that looked comfortable, testing whether I could make it look chic as well.

Enjoy a day on the town in a man's lightweight suit. Give it feminine style by rolling sleeves and tying on a sweatshirt.

What follows are descriptions of menswear pieces that I found instantly adaptable, along with ideas on how to wear them. Take the suggestions as they are or use them to spark designs of your own.

MEN'S FORMAL WEAR

For spring and summer, try this beautiful look on the cheap. Wear a man's white dinner jacket over a white tube skirt, teamed with a camisole, blouse, and pearls. In winter, try the same idea in black, even adding a cummerbund.

My husband's white dress and tuxedo shirts were real standbys. I wore them everywhere—from the beach to the office to black-tie affairs. They are adaptable to all kinds of looks and are especially comfortable, being crisp and (usually) cotton.

THE TUXEDO SHIRT GOES HAWAIIAN

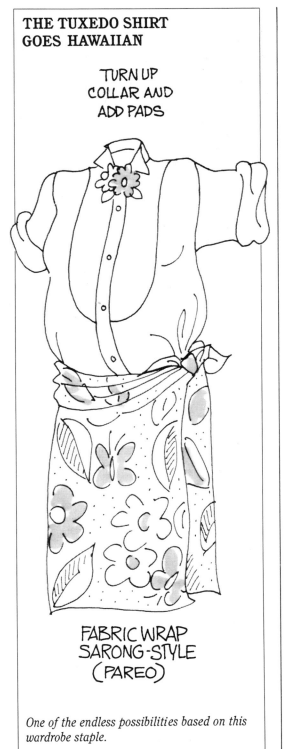

TURN UP COLLAR AND ADD PADS

FABRIC WRAP SARONG-STYLE (PAREO)

One of the endless possibilities based on this wardrobe staple.

You'll see them crop up often throughout this book.

For example, a favorite casual look for summer made use of the tuxedo shirt. (A dress shirt would work just as well.) The shirt (with shoulder pads, of course) went on top, knotted under my belly and bloused a little bit, as shown at left. Then I wrapped a pareo—a 72-inch length of 36-inch-wide fabric—at my hips, tying it on the side, sarong style. I turned up the shirt collar, rolled up the sleeves, and put on my sexy sandals. A simple, comfortable look for the price of two yards of cloth. Complete it with a matching Hepburn-style head scarf and a crownless hat, if you like.

You can also make a smart-looking dress out of a tuxedo shirt. You'll see that—and more suggestions for styling men's formal wear—in Chapter 5.

THE FEMININE DINNER JACKET

CHAIN BETWEEN BUTTONS

CUMMERBUND AT WAIST (OR BELOW)

Soften it with a camisole and pearls.

Make His Boxers Briefer

One great source of comfort clothing from the men's department is boxer shorts. They're cheap and soft and come in all sorts of wonderful colors and prints. Sew up the fly and cuff the legs. Like T-shirts (turn back to Chapter 2 for ideas on using them), dime stores sell boxer shorts for peanuts in packages of three. Wear them early in your pregnancy with extra-large T-shirts or oxford shirts and your husband's lightweight V-neck sweaters. (Later on, you can press them into service as real underwear to protect thighs from chafing, if that becomes a problem.) Roll the legs up and the waist down, as shown, to take them from sloppy to snappy. I sometimes wore two pair at once, pulling the second pair up a little higher so the legs of the first stuck out to create a kind of ruffle.

COTTON KNIT SHIRTS

In addition to the T-shirts discussed in the previous chapter, men's turtlenecks, polo shirts, and other knit styles come in handy for their extra length and width. Always add shoulder pads and consider some alterations—*if* the shirt's owner doesn't expect it back! Cut sleeves off a turtleneck and hem the edges to create a cap effect. (This is a good idea for layering—you get extra body warmth without too much bulk in the sleeves.) Run ribbons through the front and back casings of a polo shirt—shortening the back first, if necessary—and tie at the sides to make a blouson top.

A Very Unexpected Find—Men's Bikini Underwear

The biggest surprise I stumbled upon in my husband's wardrobe was his stretch bikini underwear (the kind without the pocket). I tried on a pair one day and found them sensationally comfortable. I ended up wearing them for the rest of my pregnancy. For some reason, the legs were more comfortable than women's underwear. The fit across—or rather under—my tummy was very accommodating. I used them later to improvise a bathing suit and a romper (see Chapter 6).

MEN'S SHIRT MAKEOVERS

PADS

CUT SLEEVES LEAVING ENOUGH TO TURN AND HEM

Alter a man's turtleneck.

FLIP UP KNIT COLLARS AND DON'T FORGET PADS!

HEM IN FRONT + BACK

HUGE MEN'S SIZES GIVE GOOD LENGTH FOR CASING

Blouse a large polo shirt.

MEN'S PAJAMAS

Men's classic red-and-black checked flannel nightshirts make cozy, comfortable maternity tunics with a pair of black leggings underneath. You can sash the tunic at the hip or not. If it's long enough, add a black turtleneck, and it just might pass muster at the office.

Men's satin pajamas can be worn elegantly at home or out. They're richest-looking in deep cranberry and navy foulards. For more on dressing them up, see Chapter 5.

NIGHTSHIRT TURNED TUNIC

WEAR THE T-SHIRT FOR ADDED COLOR

ADD LEGGINGS AND SOCKS

Layer it with leggings.

Easy style from thrift-shop racks.

Thrift, Antique, and Second-Hand Stores

If borrowing from the men in your life is not practical—or not welcomed—you can still create these snappy looks at little cost by buying men's clothes at secondhand stores. The advantage is that you are free to cut, trim, or alter in any way you desire. Suits, coats, vests, sweaters—indeed, almost any article of men's clothing—can be adapted to your needs.

Needless to say, thrift and antique clothing shops are also valuable sources for secondhand women's wear. I found a wonderful dress that was perfect for tennis (see page 94) and a discarded fur jacket with damaged sleeves. I removed the sleeves and wore it over a bulky sweater—perfect!

Look for classic styles that a few alterations or accessories can transform from tired-looking to terrific.

The best strategy for thrift shopping is to find a good store located near your home or office and stop by often. Because the inventory is one-of-a-kind, you either hit the jackpot or you don't. A perfectly wonderful outfit that's on the racks one day may be gone the next. So you up your odds if you're a regular.

ADDING SNAP TO THRIFT-SHOP SUITS

Check the racks for pieces to mix and match as feminized suits. Keep an eye out for men's shirts in stripes or solids, which you can wear over T-shirts, under large men's vests and jackets, or as light jackets themselves. Buy ties that have interesting patterns and are in good condition. Give a tie a softer, more feminine feeling by keeping the top button of your shirt open at the neck and knotting the tie loosely about an inch or so below the button. Don't worry about matching. A resounding clash of color or pattern is part of the charm of this look.

Next, add suspenders. Although I wore my husband's, I've seen wonderfully interesting ones in thrift shops for very little money. Wear them backward for style and variety. Or, if you want something a little more feminine, make your own. Keep an eye out for unusual ribbon—embroidered, tapestry, foulard, and polka-dot—which can be made into suspenders in seconds by

---

Add Suspenders for Style

Suspenders are both fun and functional, especially when you're pregnant and no longer have a waistline to hold up your pants. For variety, wear them backward, as shown, or make your own out of colorful ribbon.

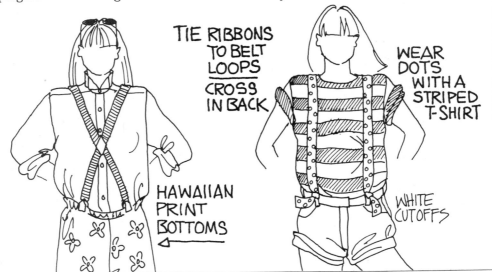

TIE RIBBONS TO BELT LOOPS — CROSS IN BACK

HAWAIIAN PRINT BOTTOMS

WEAR DOTS WITH A STRIPED T-SHIRT

WHITE CUTOFFS

simply tying pieces onto belt loops. To use ribbon with pants that have no loops, buy a package of suspender hardware in the notions department and follow instructions on the package.

If you prefer elegance to Annie-Hall charm, it's easy to achieve a classic look in suits through careful choice of color. A navy blue suit with a white shirt is instantly sophisticated. Add a red silk bow at the collar, and the whole tone changes. Imagine a brown suit with an ivory shirt and black silk bow. Or a gray suit with navy accessories, for still a different look.

If you need clothing for the weekend, you might keep your eye out for a tweed suit, then build a quintessentially English look around it. Think about adding a man's argyle pullover, oxford button-down shirt, and wonderful knit tie. Lace-up high-top shoes or loafers and a derby hat would also look great.

For summer wear, look for linen or linenlike suits in light colors and accessorize with pastel socks and suspenders, lace handkerchiefs, and flowered sneakers. I picked up several short-sleeved men's shirts in stripes and solids that I wore under big men's vests and jackets. Then I could peel off layers as the day got warmer. Often I wore two shirts at once, rolling the sleeves up so a different pattern showed. The nice thing about buying men's clothes at a thrift shop is that you're free to adjust the hems or any other part.

Secondhand stores are particularly good sources for tuxedos. As you'll see later on, I wore one often for formal affairs and was always considered appropriately dressed. In fact, I still wear them. Tuxedo jackets don't always have to be worn with matching pants. Dress them down with leggings or up with satin pants. Wear the jackets to work over pants or skirts.

Make a Long Vest

A long vest is handy to have and easy to make out of a thrift-shop men's suit or sport jacket. I used a navy gabardine jacket with brass buttons and wore it with gray flannel pants in the winter, white in the summer. All you have to do is cut the sleeves off and bind back the raw edges, as shown. Create a flattering layered look by slipping it over a shirt or sweater to top off a skirt or a pair of pants. Tuck a lace handkerchief into the pocket, add an antique pin on the lapel, and you've got a great look for very little money.

CUT SLEEVES LEAVING JUST ENOUGH TO TURN UNDER

BIND, TURN AND SEW

P.S. DON'T USE A VALUABLE JACKET FOR THIS PROJECT— HIT THE THRIFT SHOPS (MENS SECTION OF COURSE)

MEN'S SECOND-HAND OUTERWEAR

Never bypass the men's overcoat section of a thrift store. You may well find the answer to your winter overcoat problem there. Coats with raglan sleeves are especially promising because they are easy to retailor. You can add shoulder pads and shorten the sleeves. (Other ideas are given in Chapter 7.) Spend the money you save on a beautiful fur fling to wrap around your neck. You'll feel like a million dollars all winter and continue to enjoy the luxe look long after the baby is born.

Men's raincoats are worth considering, too. Trench coats can be turned into double-breasted maternity coats by simply snipping off the belt loops. You'll get a classic coat that's always in style. A great casual look can be created by denim jackets in extra-large sizes. Because denim becomes better-looking with age, secondhand or used jackets are actually preferable to new.

A man's smoking jacket or robe with a satin collar, if you are lucky enough to find one, can be worn elegantly at home or out with a pair of silk pajama pants. Or it can be made into an evening dress (see directions on page 84).

ALL MANNER OF ACCESSORIES

Don't miss the accessories counter of your thrift or antique clothing shop. Sort through those baskets or bins. At one time or another you may be lucky enough to come across lace and leather gloves, silk scarves in all shapes and sizes, earrings, bracelets, necklaces, cuff links, brooches, hats, lace collars and cuffs, wonderful old leather bags, fur muffs, or clip-on buckles and bows to dress up a pair of pumps. (See Chapter 8 for specific tips on putting your finds to work.)

Once you begin canvasing secondhand stores, it may become something of an obsession. You might find yourself dropping in well after the baby is born. Don't fight the urge—it's a wonderful way to be creative at next to no expense.

Discount Stores

The discount store is as rich and rewarding—and as inexpensive—as the secondhand store. If you haven't been in one of those large chain stores that used to be called five-and-dimes lately, take yourself on a tour. The shelves are stocked with everything from beach thongs to plastic plants. It's amazing how many useful items you'll find, at prices that are sensibly low. The appeal of discount shopping—especially when you're pregnant—is simple: If you have the urge for something new, you can satisfy it without ruining your budget.

Of course, the key to *shopping* discount is to avoid *looking* discount. The best way to do this is to buy with an idea in mind. Envision a particular outfit you'd like to create. You probably won't be buying the whole ensemble at the discount store; you'll be searching for that special something that will pull it all together. Prepare for your shopping trip by looking through fashion magazines. Take note of the color mixes, how accessories are used, the way scarves are tied, the shapes of hats. Then, when you shop, try to match magazine ideas to what's in the store. Discount stores are known for imitating the latest

Two Sweatshirt Creations

I made good use of two types of sweatshirts I found on the discount shelves. One design that's easy to make and even easier to love is the sailor-style sweatshirt. I like it best in classic red, white, or navy. As illustrated, start by sewing a double row of brass buttons down the front. Add a double stripe of grosgrain ribbon on the arm and a nautical appliqué above.

PADS

STRAW HAT

GOLD MILITARY TYPE BUTTONS

WHITE TUBE SKIRT

Make the shoulders bolder with a pair of shoulder pads. Team the top with a matching or contrasting skirt, and finish with a laquered straw hat.

For a more casual sweatshirt outfit, above, wear the standard gray, zippered kind with a tube skirt—or sweatpants—and bright T-shirt or tank top.

All the notions and accessories you need for these two outfits—except perhaps the skirts—can be found in most discount shops.

trends as soon as they appear. And chances are good you'll find something similar to the more expensive magazine version.

Other secrets I have learned for putting together a chic look at a low price are:

• Buy solid colors that are traditionally considered rich, such as beige, black, white, navy, and brown.

• Choose bright colors as accessories only: a red bag with an all-black outfit, lime-green gloves with a navy coat, a yellow scarf with a white jacket.

• Don't buy just one plastic bangle—buy six. More looks richer.

• Realize that not everything in a discount store is a wise buy. Beware of shoes that can damage your feet, off-season colors, and too much plastic.

Once you get the knack of discount shopping, you'll find it lots of fun. Every time my stepdaughter, Sophie David, comes to the States, she reignites her love affair with the American five-and-dime. As a fashion stylist for American *Elle*, she works with clothes by all the top designers. But when it comes to shopping for herself, she prefers the five-and-dime for sneakers, gold and silver slippers, tank tops, backpacks, plastic jewelry, and especially printed cotton underwear, which she says is the best anywhere.

When I was pregnant, I found discount stores invaluable. Many of the ideas you'll see throughout this book were inspired by and make use of articles purchased there. Discount extra-large thermal underwear, men's T-shirts and boxer shorts, sweatshirts, plastic rain jackets, cloth shoes, slippers, patterned socks, straw hats and berets, gloves, mittens, scarves, and hair accessories became staples in my wardrobe.

Sporting Goods Stores

When some people travel, they make sure to find the best restaurants, the most scenic sites, or the most renowned historical landmarks. My aim is always for the local sporting goods shops. I'm especially fond of Italian and French ones, but I've found interesting shops in the States, too.

True sports clothes tend to be pretty basic, which is their beauty. Simply shaped, with a minimum of detail, they're a perfect foil for all kinds of accessories. You won't find major fashion trends, but sporty looks stand the test of time. Neutral, classic colors are always well represented—plenty of tan, navy, hunter green—which means pieces can mix easily with one another. A nice plus.

Be sure to look for pullovers, shirts, shorts, pants, and jackets. When mixing sports clothes with other pieces, keep fabric weights similar—cottons with cottons, wools with wools—for the most pulled-together appearance.

I collect hats, and some of my best came from sporting goods stores. Fishing, hunting, baseball, and skiing are all sports that require great hats! Look around and you'll find more bounty—bandannas, backpacks, duffle bags, tube socks. . . .

Many of my ideas for outerwear during pregnancy also came from sporting goods shops. See Chapter 7 for more on those. I consider one rainwear outfit a high point of my shopping explorations. It kept me dry in high style for the whole nine months and thereafter. I got many smiles and compliments, and the total cost was around the price of a pair of tennis shoes.

Getting into Uniforms

Look in your local telephone directory for listings of uniform stores. These shops carry everything from domestic service to mechanical to medical uniforms, and they are some of the most unexpected—and practical—sources of maternity wear I found. Here are a few examples.

CHEFS' SHIRTS

One night at a restaurant, I noticed how crisp and cool a chef's shirt looked, and I ran out to buy one the next day. It's really nothing more than a white cotton shirt with a natty double-breasted front, easy-to-roll sleeves, and plenty of room around the waist. I wore mine in many different ways, but always with shoulder pads, to make it look less like a uniform. Teaming the shirt with navy shorts and red suspenders was a good idea. For fun, I wore it with big men's madras shorts and orange suspenders. Those are both casual looks. But if you press the shirt well, you can even wear it to work by buttoning it over any skirt you like. Add a few strands of pearls or a bright silk scarf around the neck to dress it up a few notches more. Adding trim, such as ruffles or braid, and new buttons, can also create different moods. You can even add fabric to the bottom to make a dress.

Dentists' shirts are another great find from uniform stores, similar to chefs' shirts but lighter weight and with short sleeves. (You've probably spent some time staring up at them with your mouth full of instruments.) Cuff the sleeves and wear them

A chef's shirt teamed with men's shorts for warm-weather comfort.

plain with shorts and suspenders, or decorate them using variations on the chef's shirt ideas.

LAB COATS

I had never really noticed lab coats before I became pregnant, but once I started making regular visits to the doctors' offices, my lab-coat awareness increased. Best bought in large sizes that settle easily around you, these lightweight coats can be worn as long jackets over skirts or pants. They're also good as light wraps for outdoors or as cover-ups on the beach. If you prefer your jackets shorter, just hem the bottom to the length you like. As always, shoulder pads are an important

Chef's Shirt Chic

Buy a chef's shirt at a uniform shop (check your phone book) and style it in one of these ways:

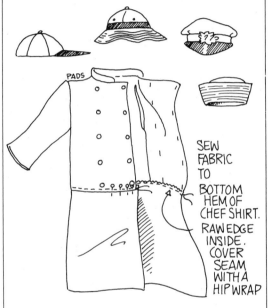

SEW FABRIC TO BOTTOM HEM OF CHEF SHIRT. RAW EDGE INSIDE. COVER SEAM WITH A HIP WRAP

- Create a dress by pinning a length of fabric to the hem and topstitching. Hide the seam with a hip wrap. Top it all off with a whimsical hat, according to your mood.

MAKE A CUFF

GOLD BRAID AND BRASS BUTTONS

- Add braid trim and brass buttons for a Russian flavor.

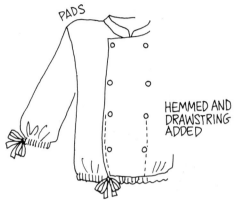

PADS

HEMMED AND DRAWSTRING ADDED

- Make casings at the hem and the wrists, and add drawstrings to give blousiness.

MULTI COLORED BUTTONS IN PAIRS!

BUTTONS

CHANGE BUTTONS TO: BRASS OR ANTIQUE, PLASTIC IN FUNNY SHAPES, OR CHILDREN'S MOTIFS →

- Replace boring buttons—use some with pizzazz.

The lab coat—a crisp, cool cover-up.

addition for style and definition. Other changes are limited only by your ingenuity. You can leave the lab coat white or dye it. Change the buttons. Sew a military appliqué on the pocket or wear it as a summer evening coat, gluing fake colored jewels all over in a random design. The variations are virtually endless.

JUMPSUITS

Uniform stores also offer great deals on jumpsuits, which may go by the name of coveralls. Look for those made for gas-station attendants, orderlies, and flight crews. (You may also find great silky para-

chuter's jumpsuits at army/navy stores.) Most snap or zip up the front, have elastic at the back of the waist, and sport plenty of pockets. They don't pull, bind, or require any decision making. Simply put one on, roll up the sleeves and cuffs, add key accessories, and you're dressed.

The jumpsuit I brought home was blue, but they come in a slew of colors. I wore mine with sleeves rolled to three-quarter length, then pushed up above the elbows. I rolled up the pant legs to show my lace stockings underneath and left the front undone a bit to reveal a hint of camisole. Then I put on lots of necklaces and a stack of bangles on each wrist. A sexy and wonderfully comfortable look for next to nothing. Try it—or some of the other variations shown at right.

Mechanics' overalls have easy appeal for everyday wear.

Jazz Up a Jumpsuit

Uniform stores are great sources for roomy jumpsuits—the ones that mechanics, flight crews, and even parachutists wear. Here are some ways to make them fashionable.

SHOW YOUR CAMISOLE

SHOW YOUR LACE STOCKINGS

- For summer, cut off sleeves and legs and roll them up—no need to finish the edges.

LARGE SIZE JUMPSUIT WITH ELASTIC AT BACK

(UN-ZIP AS YOU GROW)

LAYER WITH TURTLENECKS AND T-SHIRTS

TAPER PANTS AND ROLL

- Add lace stockings, camisole, and jewelry for a feminine feeling.

- In cooler weather, add layers underneath and gather the legs into warm socks.

Import Shop Options

When Dr. Dale Abadir, a dermatologist from New Rochelle, New York, was pregnant, she wore intricately embroidered Egyptian caftans for special occasions. A housewife and mother of three turned Indian saris into colorful gowns. An editor who answered my questionnaire bought three sets of Chinese pajamas to wear around the house. And a television reporter lived—and worked—in loose, flowing Indian dresses.

All of these ideas came from the small import shops you'll find in most major cities. They often carry wicker or rattan furniture, ceramic vases, and brass incense burners, in addition to dresses, skirts, and tops. Many of the clothes are big, billowy, and perfectly suited to pregnant bodies. Their prices are low, and the fabrics from which they're made are pure and natural.

Some pieces can be found in specialty catalogs and department stores. And if you're lucky enough to travel, you can pick them up at their sources. But by and large, the tiny hole-in-the-wall shops are still your best bet for authentic pieces at rock-bottom prices. For a less exotic feeling, stick to simple, solid colors like white, black, red, and navy.

I fell in love with kimonos on a trip to Japan and have collected them ever since. They're made in wonderfully feminine fabrics, like fine cottons, which feel good on your body. I thought I'd have to go back to Japan to get some more just as nice, but I was wrong. Local Japanese import shops carry kimonos similar to the ones I got in Japan.

Kimonos combine Far Eastern flair with classic comfort.

Tops are always in short supply when you're pregnant. So when I saw a display of "happy" coats while shopping in a Chinese import store one day, I was immediately interested. These look like hip-length kimonos. When I saw the price—quite reasonable—I decided to bring a few home. My favorite adaptation was to sew a strip of Indian gauze along the bottom edge, as shown on page 57, to create a hip wrap. When you put it on, tie the sash tightly around your hips—in back or under your belly—and blouse the jacket above it. The bold colors are a real lift, and the hip wrap makes a flattering narrow line. All you need to add is a knit tube or straight skirt. If the front gapes, secure it with a decorative pin, or if you prefer, wear a camisole or a tank top underneath. You can also tie the jacket on over a knit dress for the same great effect.

Quick Chic—
The Kimono Dress

One of the best ways to adapt a kimono is to hand-sew it down the front for an instant dress. Here's how:

- Place right sides of front edges together and sew up to where your breast bone will be.

- Turn right-side-out and slip on over your head. Hem if desired.

Once that's done, you can create a multitude of different looks. Layer pants and shirts underneath. Sash the hips. Or gather the sleeves up with ribbon or shoelaces, as shown.

In warm weather, there's no cooler clothing under the sun than the kimono. I can vouch for that. My daughter was born midsummer, and kimonos got me through the last month.

RIGHT SIDES TOGETHER
PIN AND SEW UP TO YOUR BREAST BONE

RIGHT SIDE OUT
SEWN UP

ROLL

TIE UP SLEEVES

Oriental Adaptations

Import shops often carry embroidered Chinese jackets like the one shown at the left. Buy a large one and wear it open over a T-shirt.

Check your phone directory for shops that sell karate uniforms. The jackets are wonderfully adaptable because the ties at the sides can be adjusted as you grow.

KARATE JACKET

TIES AT SIDES: INFINITELY ADJUSTABLE TO CHANGE AS YOU CHANGE

SKINNY BLACK TUBE SKIRT OR LEGGINGS

BALLET SLIPPERS

CHINESE MARY JANES

ESPADRILLES

CHINESE HAPPY JACKET

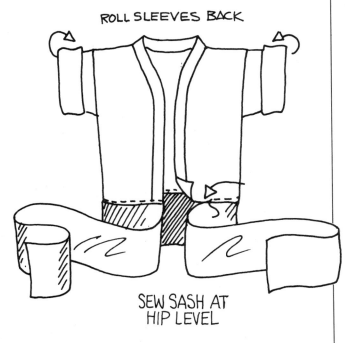

ROLL SLEEVES BACK

SEW SASH AT
HIP LEVEL

AND TIE BEHIND IN A KNOT-
TUCK ENDS IN OR NOT.

Add a hip sash to a Chinese happy jacket, leaving long ends that you can wrap in front and tie in back.

In addition to happy jackets, you'll often find Chinese shirts with mandarin collars made of cotton or silk. They are usually quilted and carry embroidered designs and braid trim. Buy one of these in the largest size you can find. Transform it into a jacket by adding shoulder pads. Then, put the jacket over a cotton T-shirt and tube skirt.

For a casual evening, take a Chinese jacket made of satin—the traditional quilted kind with frog closings—and tuck it into a pair of Indian dhoti pants. The shape of these pants—wide on top, with a drawstring waist, and narrow at the ankles—makes them great choices for pregnant bodies. Wear dhotis under any other long top or jacket, just as you would regular pants or leggings. For an accentuated ethnic feeling, cut a caftan to knee length and wear it over the pants. This is a good look for at home or weekend, and it's as comfortable as pajamas.

Karate jackets can be purchased at sporting goods stores or karate institutes. Wear them with tube skirts or bright leggings—or the roomy, calf-length, elasticized or drawstring-waist pants they come with. You might also wear a karate jacket with a pair of Indian dhoti pants.

From your husband's closet to uniform shops to import stores, let searching out alternative pieces for your pregnancy wardrobe take you far afield of your usual shopping grounds. Think of it as an adventure. You never know what wonderful piece or incredible bargain is waiting inside the next door. Happy hunting!

CHAPTER 4

Maintaining Your Professional Image

It's ironic, but true. Just when it's more important than ever to look professional, being pregnant makes it harder than ever. Let's face it, old prejudices die hard. There are plenty of people all too willing to assume that becoming pregnant means you've dropped out of professional competition. It's up to you to prove otherwise.

Keeping up your appearance is one potent way to show that work remains a priority. As image consultant and author Emily Cho has said: "Clothes are a visible clue to your state of mind. By emphasizing the positive aspects of yourself through your dress, you can inspire confidence in your abilities and judgment." It's sort of a self-fulfilling prophecy. If you look like you mean business, people expect you to perform well—and so you do. And clothes can be used symbolically to your advantage. A friend of mine bought herself a spanking new—and quite expensive—attaché case in her eighth month. Whether she was conscious of it or not, that attaché was saying, "I'll be back!" After all, you don't make that kind of investment and then let it gather dust in the closet.

There are other important reasons to dress attractively at this special time. As you get bigger, you may begin to feel awkward and a bit self-conscious about your appearance, much as you love being pregnant. Choosing clothes that make you feel really good, and paying attention to details like making sure your nails are perfectly polished and your lipstick on straight, can do a lot to offset any negative feelings you may have. And the effort you make is repaid in admiring looks and positive feedback, both of which are great for boosting your confidence—just when you need it most.

How you decide to treat your pregnancy depends on you and your individual work situation. You may feel it's in your best interest to keep the pregnancy under wraps as long as you can. There are several reasons for this. A prevailing one is that the later you announce your pregnancy, the shorter the pregnancy—and subsequent leave—will seem to co-workers and bosses. Another has to do with office politics: One woman I spoke with kept her pregnancy a secret for five and a half months because she felt that the promotion she was waiting for might go to someone else if it were known she was expecting. Third, there are the physical reasons. Some women prefer to wait until the high-risk first trimester is over. And others choose to wait until they get back the results of their amniocentesis—usually during the fifth month. For all of these reasons, career consultant and *Glamour* job columnist Marilyn Moats Kennedy recommends not wearing maternity clothes until you absolutely have to. As Kennedy points out: "If you're dressed professionally, most people will hesitate to ask if you're pregnant. You might have just gained weight—and no one wants to risk mentioning your increased girth if you haven't offered a reason."

If you work in a more casual environment, you may feel free to announce your pregnancy relatively early. In that case, your clothing alternatives are not as rigid or demanding. You can have more fun being flexible with your changing shape—emphasizing your expanding tummy with hip wraps and using the ideas suggested in Chapter 3 on alternative shopping. Study the T-shirt options given in Chapter 2, as well. They can carry you from suit to jeans and add colorful variety to the most often-worn pants and skirts.

Every company has its own psychology and traditions. In general, it's best to take your cues from co-workers and follow your own gut feelings. Just remember, there is no such thing as dressing in a neutral way. One way or the other, you will be making a statement. Read on for ways to look terrific, no matter what kind of work you do.

Clothes That Keep Your Secret

If you do need—or choose—to keep your pregnancy to yourself for a while, it is not terribly difficult until about the fourth month—and even a little later if your weight gain is minimal. Advice I heard again and again among the women I surveyed was how important it is to introduce any new garments you buy very gradually. Showing up at work in a parade of new outfits is a clear signal that something in your life has changed. And it won't take your co-workers long to deduce what it is. Keep questions to a minimum by keeping a low wardrobe profile.

Mary Jane Berrien, travel advertising manager for *Fortune* magazine, found that buying a few new items one size larger than usual and very much like her existing work clothes helped allay suspicions. Mary Jane typically wore suits and dresses made of very good wool during the winter, so early on in her pregnancy she picked up several varieties of wool at a fabric shop and had a dressmaker make some very simple, roomy dresses for her. It was the fifth month before anyone guessed that Mary Jane was pregnant.

How do you manage a gradual introduction of a few new items when everything suddenly starts feeling tight at once? Chances are you'll feel the pinch in your skirts first. But before you relegate them to storage, flip back to page 28 for easy ways to add inches at the waist. Straight skirts are especially flattering now. The narrow bottoms make your whole silhouette look slimmer. All you have to do is hide the altered waistline.

EXPAND A FAVORITE BLOUSE

OPEN SIDE SEAMS AND HOLD THEM TOGETHER WITH ELASTIC OR RIBBONS

HIDE GAPS WITH A LOOSE-FITTING JACKET. REMEMBER TO CREATE A LONG LINE WITH SKIRT, HOSE, AND SHOES IN THE SAME DARK TONE.

Cover the gaps with a loose jacket.

Sometimes you can increase the wear you get out of a garment just by changing the way you wear it: Instead of tucking in your tops, switch to long sweaters you can slide over your skirts. Or mask a too-tight blouse by wearing a vest on top. This can be done winter and summer: When it's cold, choose a wool vest. When it's warm, select a cotton one. If it makes you more comfortable, leave a few blouse buttons undone under the vest. Who's to know?

If your favorite silk blouse still fits across the bust but is straining across your middle, open the side seams partway up, as shown, and use elastic or ties to hold the sides together. Wear the blouse over your skirt, if it's cut straight across the bottom, and hide the sides under your jacket.

Make Suits and Jackets Grow With You

Suits, and less formal outfits pulled together by jackets, are the standard wardrobe for women in many offices. They look tidy and professional and are very versatile, and you can create different looks by changing blouses, jewelry, scarves, and other accessories. If your wardrobe already consists of suits and jackets, you can continue to wear them in early- to mid-pregnancy with just a few alterations. Here are some suggestions.

Take advantage of the fact that jackets are perfect for camouflage. (Consider the streamlining effect they have on men with potbellies!) Some jackets look fine unbuttoned, especially the rather long, unconstructed types. Many of these don't even have buttons. Their length serves to hide the waist-stretchers I've suggested, and they are not restricting in front. The vertical lines formed by their open lapels help mask your expanding waistline. These jackets come in wool, cotton, linen, or gabardine—various fabric weights that can serve in various seasons. Add them to drop- or no-waisted dresses, too, to give a more formal, businesslike appearance.

If you have more fitted jackets that are meant to be buttoned, don't put them away yet. You can get at least an extra month of wear out of your single-breasted jacket by moving the buttons over an inch or so for a more comfortable fit. And before you retire your too-tight double-breasted blazer, try one of these two tricks:

• Turn the jacket into a more roomy single-breasted one by moving one set of buttons over to the inside edge, opposite the row of buttonholes.

• Move both sets of buttons to the inside edges of the jacket. Position one set near the outside edges of the buttonholes so they camouflage them. Then loop "gold" chain necklaces—bought inexpensively at a five-and-dime store—from the buttons on one side to the buttons on the other (see illustration below). To shorten the chain to fit, double or triple it across the buttons, use a shorter bracelet-length chain, or remove links with needle-nose pliers.

As you grow, think about the menswear ideas presented in Chapter 3. Depending on the atmosphere of your workplace, you may be able to switch to men's suits and jackets when yours just won't do anymore.

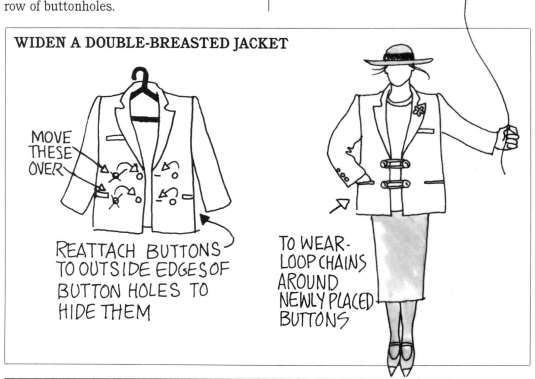

WIDEN A DOUBLE-BREASTED JACKET

MOVE THESE OVER

REATTACH BUTTONS TO OUTSIDE EDGES OF BUTTON HOLES TO HIDE THEM

TO WEAR- LOOP CHAINS AROUND NEWLY PLACED BUTTONS

Shortcuts to a Pulled-Together Wardrobe

The perfectly accessorized looks that appear on the fashion pages of magazines are rarely as spontaneous as they seem. Most are the result of an editor's spending hours trying this sock with that shoe, this bracelet with that earring. Then, when she's got it exactly right, she photographs all of the pieces together, files the photo, and takes it out on location as a reference while the model is being dressed. So much for improvisational magic.

Often, working women expect dressing to be as easy as adding up a column of figures. But the best looks take time and thought—something few people have patience for at seven o'clock in the morning on a workday. Much better to set aside a few hours on a Saturday and really concentrate on the clothes and accessories you have. This is doubly important in planning a pregnancy wardrobe, because you're struggling not only to look great but also to keep up with your body's changes. By playing around with all the pieces at once, you're likely to fall into some ideas you'd never have thought of while the clock was ticking and your mind was geared to the day ahead. A few possibilities are suggested on pages 68–69.

Most women need five or six different outfits for the office. Once you've used the ideas already presented here to get several looks set, find a useful way to record them. The simplest is a list, but the best is to arrange all of the pieces of the outfit on the floor or bed in a reasonable facsimile of the way you'll be wearing them—the scarf tied at the neck, the pin on the lapel, etc. Then take individual Polaroids of each outfit. Include every detail—from the blouse to the stockings to the shoes and jewelry. Then keep the information handy for morning reference.

Depending on the range of your work activities, it may be helpful to note which look works best for a particular purpose. One outfit might be terrific for meetings, others for presentations, entertaining, or traveling. This advance planning takes a little time at the outset, but it saves in the long run. And how nice to avoid the daily panic, wondering if you've got the right thing to wear.

The sifting-out process may also turn up some holes in your wardrobe—well in advance of that rushed workday morning. You may discover that you don't have the black stockings you need to add finish to a certain dress. Or it may occur to you that one new pair of black patent heels would answer most of your shoe needs. Or that one print scarf could pull a whole new outfit together. Once you note the omissions, you can keep them in mind the next time you're out shopping.

When you shop for new pieces, remember that the most versatile wardrobes are those that include the least number of colors. Especially when you're pregnant, and your wardrobe is more limited, it's important to select a basic color scheme and stick to it. If you restrict what you buy to red, white, and navy, for instance—with a few accent colors and neutrals added—everything in your wardrobe will work together, thus multiplying your options. It's advice that's apt for every budget. During her pregnancies, Catherine Alain-Bernard, editor-in-chief of *Elle* magazine in Paris and mother of two, chose to wear a

A Shortcut Maternity "Skirt"

Maternity skirts are handy to have, but expensive, and useful for only a few months. Here's an inexpensive alternative that requires a bare minimum of sewing and time. It's the brainstorm of my friend model-designer-mom Yvonne Tozzi from Australia.

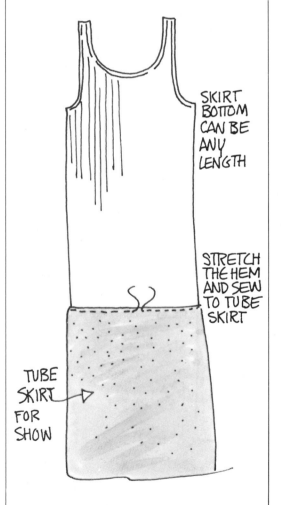

SKIRT
BOTTOM
CAN BE
ANY
LENGTH

STRETCH
THE HEM
AND SEW
TO TUBE
SKIRT

TUBE
SKIRT
FOR
SHOW

LAYER
SHIRTS
AND TUNICS
OVER IT

You'll need a long man's tank undershirt and a piece of 36-inch-wide knit fabric long enough to wrap loosely around your hips. The tank will stretch down over your tummy, with the fabric skirt beginning at your hips so that it can fall close to your legs rather than billow out. It's much more comfortable than a real skirt, since it hangs from your shoulders—not your disappearing waist.

Sew the fabric edges together to create a wide tube. Stretching the tank to match the width of the fabric tube, pin and sew the "skirt" on. Pin the hem to the length desired and sew. Wear the garment as a skirt-and-undershirt, topping it with long shirts, altered blouses, and jackets or cardigans.

lot of black. According to Catherine, "I always felt more professional dressed in black." So unless you have plenty of disposable income, be disciplined about what you buy. Much as you may pine for that kelly-green jacket, pass it by if it doesn't go with anything else you own. If you're in the mood for kelly green, buy a scarf or hat in that color. At least you can wear them beyond the nine months of your pregnancy.

Increasing Your Top Options

You can get a lot of mileage out of just a couple of skirts and pants and a jacket when you change the look with tops. A T-shirt, a cotton button-down, and a silk blouse teamed with the same classic skirt create three very different moods. As I mentioned in the last chapter, crisp men's shirts are a terrific resource throughout your pregnancy. Worn under a suit and accessorized in a feminine way, they can easily pass muster at work. If you can wear pants, try this classic and classy look: Put his big navy-blue golf cardigan (if your husband doesn't own one, it may be a worthwhile purchase) over a white shirt and navy or plaid pants (maternity, or men's pants held with suspenders). Add a strand of pearls. Perfect.

Adding interest at the neck is always an excellent strategy. It sets off your face and draws the eye away from the stomach area, where you don't want anyone's attention focused. If your neck is long and thin, add some substance with a turtleneck (pulled up all the way), discrete ruffles, or turned-up collars accessorized in different ways. Shorter necks benefit from V-necklines, which create a long vertical line. See the illustrations on page 67 for specific ideas.

I've already discussed the versatility of T-shirts and other casual tops, but at work most women need something a bit dressier. Here are two answers that offer class without high cost.

TWO SILK-SCARF TOPS

Nothing dresses up a suit or coordinated skirt and jacket like a silk blouse. When it comes to professional polish, silk is right up there with Chanel pumps and pearls. When my best friend called me in a panic because she had an important meeting to attend and no top to wear with her suit, I told her about this series of tops that are extravagant in every way except price. The secret is silk scarves. If you own some, the tops below are yours for the tying. No sewing required. If you don't, they'll be a wonderful investment you don't have to pack away when the baby's born.

With its soft draping at the neck, the cowl-neck scarf top gives any suit instant sophistication. You'll need two scarves, each 45 inches square or larger. The scarves needn't match; a print and solid combination is fine. Placing the wrong sides of the scarves together, tie the top right and left ends, as shown on page 66, to create the neck opening. Place the scarves over your head and knot the bottom ends over each hip. Slip on your jacket and arrange the cowl in soft folds. Since the sides are open, there's lots of room for expansion and plenty of breathing room. And the bottom of the front scarf can be pulled down to camouflage your waistline. The jacket hides the knots. For all the world knows, you have just treated yourself to a fabulous silk blouse.

The v-neck scarf top looks even more like a bonafide suit blouse and is sexy and professional to boot. You'll need three scarves, each 45 inches square or larger. Lay the one you want for the back on a flat surface, right side down. Fold the remaining two scarves into triangles, as shown, with the right sides facing out, and place them on the top of the "back" scarf, as illustrated. Tie knots at the top and put the blouse on. Crossing the scarves in front to create a V, tie at each hip. Secure the neck opening with a small safety pin under the front flap. Be creative with the scarves you choose. You may want to use all solids or

TIE ON A V-NECK SCARF TOP

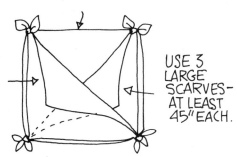

USE 3 LARGE SCARVES— AT LEAST 45" EACH.

TIE OR PIN AT SHOULDERS — WEAR OVER A CAMISOLE AND UNDER A JACKET

CREATING THE COWL-NECK SCARF TOP

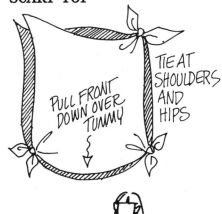

PULL FRONT DOWN OVER TUMMY

TIE AT SHOULDERS AND HIPS

Remember to keep your jacket on to hide the gaps.

all prints. Or you may want to mix them so that one flap is solid, the other print. In this way, you can create a week's worth of tops or more—all different.

A slight disadvantage to the scarf tops is that, since the sides are open, your jacket must stay on all day. Of course, this is also what makes the tops so comfortable. If the bareness bothers you, slip a camisole on underneath. If you want to be able to take off your jacket, simply sew up side seams by hand or machine, leaving openings for the arms.

The Neckline Story

A flattering neckline puts the focus on your face, drawing attention away from your expanding tummy. Here's how to choose the best for you.

- You can lengthen the look of a short neck by wearing Vs. Carrying the line of skin from your face past your neck (but not too low at the office!) emphasizes the vertical.

- Long, thin necks need the added volume of a turned-up collar, turtleneck, or scarf. Men's white shirts come in handy at work (turn collars up!), and you can accessorize them to create all manner of moods.

- For short necks:

- For long necks:

What Works at Work

Creating the perfect look for meetings, travel, and client lunches takes some advance planning. Spend a Saturday morning trying out various combinations from your wardrobe.

Pull it *all* together—from earrings and hair accessories to hose and shoes. New possibilities will be re-

JACKET AND SKIRT IN BLACK WOOL KNIT-CHARCOAL GRAY TURTLE-NECK. GOLD JEWELRY. BLACK BOW IN YOUR HAIR

PROPORTION IS EVERYTHING!

A GREAT PIN

DARK LEGS, FEET AND DRESS (ALL THE SAME COLOR)

vealed, and you'll see clearly what small items you could purchase to make it all gel.

Here are examples of ensembles that work, from conservative to casual. At far left, black and gray de-emphasize width, while gold jewelry adds a spark. Next, a fabulous scarf and pin add pizzazz to a dark sweater dress. A scarf also perks up a neutral-colored suit—without compromising its professional tone. Finally, at far right, a karate jacket and knit pants make a chic ensemble for a less formal workplace.

USE A CLIP EARRING AND 2 SHOELACES TIED AT THE NAPE FOR LENGTH

BIG SCARF WITH A MUTED PATTERN IN NEUTRAL COLORS

SUBSTITUTE BIG BUTTONS FOR KARATE JACKET TIES

WEAR KNIT PANTS

Easy Dresses to Sew

If you have just a few extra minutes and a little sewing experience, you can make some comfortable dresses for the late months at the office.

There were two that I wore time and again. One was a shirtdress that worked beautifully in many situations. Its light weight makes it best for spring or summer wear. There's some sewing involved, but it's minimal. All you need are a man's shirt (I'm partial to tuxedo shirts for this purpose) and a length of matching or contrasting fabric to sew on at hip level, creating a skirt. If you do choose a tuxedo shirt and the bib is piqué, you may want to echo that fabric in the skirt.

Use a ruler to draw a horizontal line from one side of the shirttail slit to the other. This is your sewing line. Measure this line and add two inches to determine the length of fabric you'll need for the skirt. Pin the correct length of fabric to the sewing line with the opening in front, folding a half inch of fabric over, as shown at right. Topstitch the fabric and shirt together, then trim away the shirttail from inside. Turn the overlapping vertical edge of the skirt under about a half inch and topstitch it onto the opposite edge, leaving a slit. Hem to desired length. Cover the seam with a wide ribbon belt. Flip back cuffs and, of course, add shoulder pads.

A fall or winter look that's both easy to wear and to make is the plaid tunic. All you need are two lengths of tartan plaid. If the selvages are presentable, you can leave them as they are. If they're ragged, turn them back and topstitch. Put wrong sides

THE SHIRTDRESS—HOW TO

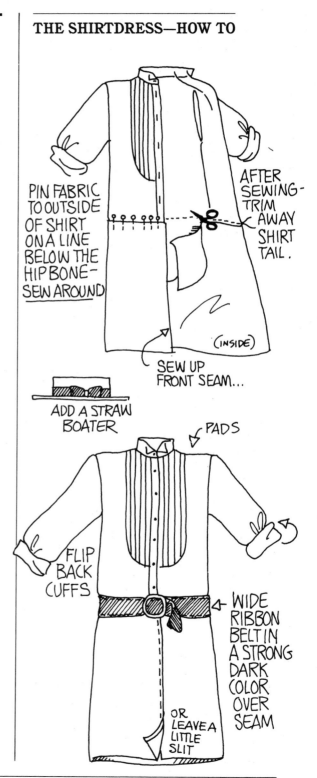

PIN FABRIC TO OUTSIDE OF SHIRT ON A LINE BELOW THE HIP BONE— SEW AROUND

AFTER SEWING— TRIM AWAY SHIRT TAIL.

(INSIDE)

SEW UP FRONT SEAM...

ADD A STRAW BOATER

PADS

FLIP BACK CUFFS

WIDE RIBBON BELT IN A STRONG DARK COLOR OVER SEAM

OR LEAVE A LITTLE SLIT

Comfort Tips for the Working Woman

- Concentrate on extra good posture at your desk.

- Avoid large weight gains by eating sensibly.

- Put your feet up whenever you can get away with it.

- Stay away from sodas and large meals during the day.

- Workaholics: Be prepared to slow down and listen to your body to avoid stress.

- Take short breaks during the day—to stretch, get a drink of water, grab a healthy snack.

- Make a conscious effort to keep things in perspective. Your sense of humor will be a great help.

THE PLAID TUNIC

SEW 2 LENGTHS OF TARTAN PLAID AT SHOULDERS

SEW RIBBONS AND GATHER AND TIE AT HIP OR BELOW

Easy to make, and best on tall, slim figures.

together and sew a seam across the width, leaving an opening large enough to get your head through. Stitch four eight-inch lengths of grosgrain ribbon at hip level. Turn the tunic right side out, put your head through, and hem it to the desired length. Tie the ribbons at the sides. That's it! This can be worn over a knit dress or a sweater and skirt. It's a great look for the weekend, too, with pants and boots. (And of course you can make it out of fabric other than plaid.) Because it is rather bulky, the tunic dress is best on tall, slim figures.

Maternity Dress Makeovers

Especially in these last few months, when even one- or two-size-larger dresses won't do, many women turn to new or handed-down maternity dresses as working wardrobe staples. I decided to see what could be done to endow these often unsophisticated dresses with some authority and elegance. Here's a list of the types of dresses you'll find in the stores, and what you can do to add some style:

- Puff-sleeved, drop-waisted dress. Add a shirt, tie, and blazer.

LOTS OF PATTERNS— ALL MUTED

- Any plain, uninteresting dress. Lay an oversized scarf or shawl over one shoulder, cross it diagonally over the body, and anchor it with a hip wrap.

- Dress with a Peter Pan collar. Turn the collar up and secure the neck opening with a cameo.

- Dress with a ditzy bow. Remove the bow and add a bold antique brooch or cameo. Pull on a jacket joined with gold chains.

- Plain chemise. Tie on a hip wrap and add a long line with a string of pearls.

- Dress with a frilly collar. Substitute an antique lace collar. Add a long, floppy satin bow, a jacket, and a hip wrap, all in the same color.

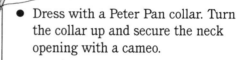

- Dress with great fabric but bad design. Change its style by adding a tie or pearls and a man's pullover.

Dresses for Success

While it may not have quite the same clout as a suit at the office, the right dress—one that's not frilly, flouncy, or otherwise inappropriate—can definitely look like it means business. If you happen to own any drop-waisted or unwaisted coatdresses, you've undoubtedly discovered their talent for concealment. If you don't, either type would be a good investment now, as you'll probably be able to wear even a non-maternity dress in those styles well into your sixth or seventh month, and possibly longer.

If it's winter, choose dresses in silk, wool gabardine, or a rich, nubby fabric. In the summer, linen or a linen blend, poplin, or seersucker will fill the bill. Keep accessories plain: Pearls or gold chains or beads are good. Avoid a wrist full of noisy bangles—which is not businesslike at any time. Keep stockings simple, matching them to the dress for a lengthening effect. If traveling is a big part of your job, keep that in mind when you shop. Look for non-wrinkling blends or knits—both look as good when you get there as when you left. And if you're called upon to attend lots of meetings, choose styles on the dressy side. Change the looks with different collars, scarves, and jewelry. The rule to remember is: Buy less, but buy better.

A coatdress is a particularly good choice to create a professional image. As

Shoe Clips— Great Boredom Breakers

A crucial part of any work wardrobe is shoes. In Chapter 8 you'll see tips on keeping feet healthy and happy as they struggle to hold your extra weight. For work purposes, if your shoe size has gone up half a size or more during pregnancy, you obviously can't continue to wear your regular closetful of pumps. However, your budget will call for you to keep shoe buying to a minimum, which can get mighty boring. The best boredom breaker I've heard of: shoe clips! Once you've got a collection, you can get by with buying one simple pair of pregnancy-size pumps in a super neutral color. Five pairs of clips yield a new pair of shoes for every day of the work week. Some women I know attach their clip earrings to their pumps. The advantage there is that you already have a bunch on hand in your jewelry box.

Quick and Classy Hairstyles

Now, more than ever, you need a hairstyle that's flattering to your face and proportions as well as easy to handle during the morning rush. It's probably best to avoid drastic changes, but do consider new bangs or a light reshaping, to wake up your old look. Here are some easy-care styles you might like to experiment with.

- For short to medium-length hair:

WISPY AND LIGHT ON TOP

COULDN'T BE EASIER!

"GAMIN" BANGS ADD SOFTNESS

NO FUSS— FINGER FLUFF

MOUSSE OFF OF YOUR FACE

WORKS WITH STRAIGHT-ENED HAIR OR HAIR WITH GREAT BODY

CROPPED SHORT AND EASY WITH A STRONG SHAPE

- For longer hair:

BEND OVER AND APPLY HAIRSPRAY—JUST UNDERNEATH

FLIP HAIR BACK AND SMOOTH WITH A BRUSH (JUST THE TOP)

MOUSSED "CAP" EAR TO EAR

PIN MOST OF YOUR HAIR AROUND A BUN FORM—USE EXTRA HAIR TO MAKE A LITTLE KNOT ON TOP (PULL THROUGH THE BUN FORM)

- For thick, curly hair:

WRAP LITTLE "EXPLOSIONS" OF HAIR ON TOP AND AS A PONYTAIL

4 COMBS MAKE A HALO OF HAIR

you sit at a desk or conference table, it looks like a suit. Underline the similarities by accessorizing it in the same way: Tuck a lace handkerchief in the pocket. Wear a pin on the lapel. Once it begins getting tight, see if you can move the buttons as described for the double-breasted jacket, page 62.

One woman I talked to hit the jackpot with three silk dresses she found in the regular dress department during her third month. All three, though different, had the same basic lines. They fell straight from the bust and got fuller toward the hem. They were in solid colors, so they could be easily accessorized to create many ensembles. Sometimes she added scarves, sometimes she wore pearls or gold beads. Although she hadn't expected them to, the dresses took her straight through to the ninth month. Since they were silk, a perfect transitional fabric, they worked for fall, winter, and spring. And they could be dressed up for important meetings and special nights. All in all, it was an investment that payed off.

A dress that served me well was a long-sleeved all-black knit shift that I bought two sizes larger than usual. I wore it with a white shirt—so that only the collar and cuffs showed—and a man's tweed jacket on top. The outfit took me to meetings, lunches, and presentations. And, since it was knit, it traveled beautifully as well.

Another knit that I turned to again and again was the white turtleneck sweater dress shown on page 58. Sashed with a black wool jersey wrap and topped with a black knit jacket, all it needed was a string of pearls and black pumps to meet any office challenge. And I could transform it easily by changing the accessories.

Turning Day into Night

It's a good idea to put some of your working wardrobe money in at least one dress meant for day but capable of going out at night—with the right accessories. Hallmarks of that kind of dress are simple, unfussy lines and a rich-looking fabric— perhaps a wool crepe A-line with a jewel neck, in a deep burgundy or black. Here's how to take your dress from day into night:

• Add a lace scarf at the neck, fastened with a cameo.

• Pile on plenty of rhinestone jewelry. (Buy it cheap at a thrift shop.)

• Pull on a pair of short black gloves. Instant cachet!

• Splurge on a pair of ultraglamorous satin shoes and sexy hose to match.

• Carry a gorgeous satin or beaded evening bag.

• If you're daring, wear a hat with a veil and lots of red lipstick.

• Attach a chiffon scarf to one shoulder with a brooch. Let the two ends float gracefully.

• Decorate your legs with a shimmery pair of silver or gold sheer hose.

Keeping your sense of style through a working pregnancy is personally rewarding as well as professionally savvy. You'll feel comfortable and confident, and your colleagues will have no doubts about your continued commitment to the job. And who knows? The wardrobe planning and ingenuity required may come in quite handy in the future.

CHAPTER 5

Puttin' On the Ritz

Going out—just the two of you—has a special poignancy now. Whether you are pregnant with your first, second, or third child, each night brings you closer to a change in your status. Undoubtedly, you and your husband are taking advantage of every opportunity to spend time together. And you're probably going out far more than you thought you would. You invent occasions, realizing that before long, making arrangements won't be quite so simple. As one new dad put it: "Now when we go out the meter's running," referring, of course, to the cost of the baby-sitter.

Being pregnant, and knowing your condition will not go unnoticed, you make a special effort when deciding what you are going to wear. "Everybody loves a pregnant woman," declared one new mom, who misses the limelight she enjoyed during her pregnancy. Added to that is the thrill you feel with each new inch pregnancy adds to your waistline. You're proud to show it off. Who wouldn't be? The days when women tried to gain as little as possible are over. Now, realizing the importance of nutrition for the budding baby, we applaud each pound (within reason, of course). For all of these reasons, it's the woman who's pregnant—and proud of it—

who many times eclipses the rest. Often, it's she who manages to look smashing in a sea of the merely well dressed. And what a coup that is.

Of course, a big factor in dressing up when you're pregnant is that of comfort. You want to look smashing, yes, but you also want to feel as good as you look. In this chapter you'll see lots of ways to be both comfortable and chic—and they don't involve major purchases.

Pregnancy, when you think about it, is really one long celebration. There's the big one at the beginning—when you announce the news. There's the even bigger one at the end—when the baby arrives. And in between, there are many smaller celebrations. So I'm a strong believer in having a wardrobe ready and waiting.

The real fun of dressing up when you're pregnant is the freedom you have. Since you can't look like everyone else, you needn't feel pressured to dress like anyone else. All eyes are on you, anyway, so you might as well give them something to look at! As French fashion designer Jean-Charles de Castelbajac says, "Pregnancy is a beautiful time for a woman, and she should play it up as much as she can." In that spirit, here are some wonderful ideas for puttin' on the ritz.

Formal Ritz

Unless you're as royally social as Princess Diana, you probably panic when an invitation calls for very formal dress. The arrival of such an invite when you're pregnant can really cause an anxiety attack. One woman I interviewed was invited to a black-tie business function when she was seven months pregnant. It was an important occasion, and she had to look good. The only thing she could think to do was buy the first decent-looking maternity gown she came across. The price tag—$250. And she wore it only once.

A shame? No question. But what else can you do? Turn to fashion brainstorming, of course.

THE SATIN POUF DRESS

I was recently reminded of a designer dress I loved years ago. It was small at the shoulders, small at the hem, and gigantic in between—like a big balloon. Can you imagine a better silhouette for a pregnant body?

Since the dress itself was long gone from the stores, I decided to recreate it. (The result is pictured on page 76.) Here's how: Starting with a twin-size satin sheet, cut a slit in the center for your head, as illustrated. Roll the edge of the slit back just enough to finish it with tiny hand stitches, and reinforce the edges of the slit with a few strong stitches. Slip the sheet on to determine how wide it should be. You'll want to cut it off at the wrists or a bit shorter, depending on your preference. Mark the spot with a pin, remove the dress, and cut to size. Then sew up the sides, right sides together, leaving room for

A Note on High Heels

Some women stop wearing heels early in their pregnancies, fearing they might lose their balance, or just feeling uncomfortable due to excess weight. Others wear four-inch heels until the end. My own preference was somewhere in the middle. For special nights, I did wear heels, but only if I knew I wasn't going to be standing all evening long. Most of the time I opted for flats. The choice is yours, within reason. What do the doctors say? Take a look at Chapter 8 for details.

SEW UP A SATIN SHEET

NECK SLIT

TURN BACK RAW EDGE AND HEM OR BIND

SEW TOGETHER WRONG SIDE OUT

TIE AT SIDES

RUN RIBBONS OR ELASTIC THROUGH HEMS OR SEW A NEW CASING IF TUNIC IS TOO LONG

A satin sheet becomes a pouf dress. The finished look is shown on page 76.

your arms, and turn right sides out. Next, thread elastic through the bottom casing and pull it tight. (With a sheet, a casing's already there, but, depending on your height and the length you like your dresses, you may have to cut and create a new casing.)

The neckline can be left as is, or you can add shoulder pads for more swank. Gathering up the fabric at the shoulders with rhinestone brooches is another possibility.

Add dark hose and sexy pumps and you've got a party dress for the price of a satin sheet.

THE FEMININE TUXEDO

The first time I had to deal with the problem of really dressing up, we were in Paris and had received an invitation to "come for dinner and please make it black tie." By then, I was an old hand at helping myself to my husband's wardrobe. He, fortunately, is the polar opposite of me when it comes to packing, tending toward too much. He had brought along two tuxedos. I decided to take the invitation literally and give the tux a go.

Styling it much the same way I did the rest of his suits, I raised the collar, rolled the shirtsleeves back over the sleeves of the jacket, and added suspenders. The biggest problem was the length of the pants. Folding them into socks was out of the question since I wanted to wear black satin heels. I fell back on a solution from modeling days: a temporary hem held with double-faced tape. Instead of a bow tie, I wore an antique garnet necklace.

The reaction was terrific. With my belly before me, and my hair behind me, I certainly wasn't mistaken for one of the boys. True, it wasn't quite as luxurious as a ball gown, but the intrigue it generated made up for that. And it served me well right up through my sixth month.

THE VERSATILE DRESS GOES GALA

When I introduced this tube dress in Chapter 2, I stressed its versatility. Now let me show you how really useful this simple dress can be.

First of all, to achieve gown length, you'll want to choose your fabric from the 60-inch-or-wider bolts. That's easy, since most dressy fabrics come in wide widths. The sewing technique is exactly the same as described on page 33: Sew a seam to create a big tube. Make a casing on top and thread elastic through. Hem the bottom and you've got a dress. Here's how to add the magic.

• Consider making the dress with two layers: the top layer of transparent tulle or lace, the underneath of a matching or contrasting lining fabric. I like the idea of beige or silver over white. Add a sash of four-inch-wide satin ribbon at the hip (wider ribbon stays in place better than narrow) and tie a bow on one side. Pin a silk flower or fancy pin in the center of the bow. Make a matching shawl from the transparent layer only and tie it over your shoulders.

Other layering ideas are emerald-green organza over matching crepe, with a black or navy sash, and pale-pink tulle over shocking-pink taffeta.

• Use black crepe for the dress—it drapes beautifully—and make the sash out of ruby-red satin.

• For a very feminine look, make the dress out of peach silk jersey sashed with a band of ivory satin.

• Go all out with silver lamé, sashed in still more lamé or black velvet ribbon.

• For spring and summer, make the dress up in a pale pastel color. Then sew—or pin—a row of small silk flowers along the elastic. For fun, add a pair of long white gloves, available at any bridal shop. If you can find lace gloves, so much the prettier!

DRESS UP THE VERSATILE DRESS

WRAP YOUR SHOULDERS IN TULLE—TIE IN A BOW AT THE SHOULDER

Float a sheer wrap over your shoulders.

Magical Makeup

It doesn't take much to give your regular makeup a magical evening twist. Here are some quick changes from Los Angeles makeup artist Chany Catala:

• Make your skin glow. Buy a container of shimmery gold powder and dust it on your shoulders, collarbone, cheekbones, and below your bottom lip.

• Make your best feature a focal point. If it's your lips, play them up to the hilt with lip liner, lipstick, and gloss. Don't make the mistake of putting equal emphasis on eyes, cheeks, and lips. What happens is that everything looks equal and no feature stands out.

• Make your lids shimmer. Highlight the center of each lid—just above the iris—with blue or violet iridescent shadow.

• Make your eyes more intriguing. Line upper and lower lids with soft black eye pencil (brown, if you're a blonde or redhead). Moisten a cotton swab and smudge the line. Finish with mascara.

THE GRACE OF KIMONO DRESSING

As I mentioned in Chapter 3, I'm hooked on the comfort and style of kimonos. Japanese import stores—the kind that sell everything from baskets to clothing—are good sources for authentic ones. I've also seen them in mail-order catalogs from such companies as The Horchow Collection and from museum shops. Magnificent old kimonos can often be found in antique clothing stores.

For evening, I go for the rich, vibrant colors of kimonos made of silk or rayon—fabrics that drape gracefully over a rounded body.

Here are some far from traditional ways to wear a kimono at night:

• Sew a solid kimono closed in front, as shown on page 55. Gather the sleeves up to the shoulders and fasten with matching rhinestone brooches or anything with some shine to it: rhinestone barrettes, gold thread, gold or silver chain, or metallic ribbon.

• Using the same sewn-up solid kimono, skip the sleeve gathering, add shoulder pads, and sash the hips with a wide satin ribbon in a wildly contrasting color. Emerald green on a navy kimono, for instance, taxicab yellow on purple, or pink on red.

• If you can't find a kimono to suit you, have one made to order. Most of the major pattern catalogs show kimonos in the lingerie section. Choose your pattern and dream fabric and take everything to a seamstress.

• Have a seamstress or tailor make buttonholes along the front band of a black silk kimono. Sew on crystal or rhinestone buttons and add shoulder pads to create a sensational evening dress special enough for any black-tie event.

• Cut a long kimono to knee length and add a contrasting or matching pair of silky pajama bottoms underneath. Pull it all together with a wide sash at the hip.

• Wear two kimonos at once: A solid color underneath, sewn up the front, and a second in a bold pattern slipped on top and allowed to flow gracefully behind you as you walk.

• Add a sexy note by placing a glimmering brooch at the lowest part of the deep V in front. Wear a lacy camisole underneath so that if the kimono shifts, the lace will be seen, not what's beneath. Or turn the kimono around to create a V in back.

Casual but Classy

Not every party calls for black-tie formality. When you want to look more casually festive, try some of the following ideas. All it takes is some improvisational magic.

PARTY PAJAMAS

I love the look of men's silk pajamas at night. They're a classic style that drapes beautifully and feels wonderful against your skin. I first got the idea when I was out buying a special pair for my father. The pajamas were made of silk jacquard—not slippery or shiny the way a lot of silk is—in an elegant shade of maroon. When I got them home, I held them up and was struck by the possibilities. Since I was going out that night, I rushed back to the store and bought another pair.

Because the fabric was so special, very little alteration was needed. I used the basics you've read about more than once now: I added shoulder pads, rolled the sleeves to three-quarter length, and pushed them up. Then, I tied the shirttails loosely under my tummy and rolled the pants to my ankles. The only accessories I needed were a pile of gold chains around my neck and a couple of bangles on my wrists. On my feet, I wore black satin ballerina slippers. The effect was quite luxurious. And you can bet I was the most comfortable person at the party that night!

After that successful debut, I played with the look a bit more. Here are some variations to try:

• Add several long strings of pearls (inexpensive dime-store strands are fine) to a pair of black silk pajamas for a very sophisticated, dramatic look.

• Wear the top as a jacket over a cotton T-shirt dressed up with rhinestones.

• Slip a man's white tuxedo shirt underneath, then roll the sleeves of the shirt into the sleeves of the pajama top.

• Change the buttons, using rhinestones or any other dressy button.

• Make drawstring bottoms by threading satin ribbon through the hems of the pants, as illustrated below. Or tie matching or contrasting ribbon in a criss-cross pattern over the pants bottoms, ballet-slipper style. Do it around the ankle only or all the way up the pant legs to your knees.

• Instead of rolling sleeves, you can thread ribbon through their hems and blouse them, as instructed for pant bottoms.

• Glue rhinestones or colored "gems" all over tops and bottoms for a really dressy look.

• For summer, remove the sleeves, turn the armhole edges under, and stitch. Wear a

TIE PANTS LEG WITH RIBBON

IF PAJAMA BOTTOMS ARE TOO LONG

RUN A RIBBON THRU THE HEM WITH A TINY SLIT AT THE SEAM

Men's pajamas, in cotton or silk, make elegant loungewear.

sleeveless leotard underneath for privacy. For an even barer look, gather up the shoulder seams and secure with matching rhinestone brooches.

I found that extra-large-sized pajamas worked best and felt most luxurious. If you are very small, do try on a few different sizes to see which one gives you the look you want. There are styles with collars and without. If you have a long, skinny neck like I do, a collar will help add some substance. But if you are short or have a short neck, choose a collarless style with a deep V to give you a longer line.

If silk costs more than you want to spend, explore other fabrics, such as rayon or some of the nicer polyesters. In silk's favor, though, is the fact that it is a natural fiber that allows your skin to breathe. The comfort helps justify the expenditure.

TURNING NIGHTGOWNS INTO NIGHTWEAR

When I was pregnant, I loved the romantic feeling of a voluminous antique nightgown I found at a Paris flea market and used as a dress. Since my ninth month was in midsummer, I reveled in the dress's cotton coolness and comfort. You can find similar ones at secondhand shops here. If you can't find old ones, take a look at the new nightgowns that copy antique styles. Many are both opaque and roomy enough to wear outside the house. To tame the fullness, simply add a pastel satin sash at the hip. To cut down on the see-through quality, add a full-length slip, or a camisole and half-slip, underneath. Wear ballerina flats on your feet. You really can't find a prettier look—and practical, too. After the baby is born, this dress can go right back to nightgown status.

For a sleeker, more sophisticated look, check out the loungewear collection designed by Fernando Sanchez. Many of his designs have pregnant-friendly details like wrap, drawstring, and elastic waists. The fabrics, colors, and silhouettes he uses are quite sensational-looking and would hardly be mistaken for sleepwear. Yet, because they fall into a loungewear category, the prices are not what they would be if they were sold as evening clothes. A good deal.

A COATDRESS A LA NOEL COWARD

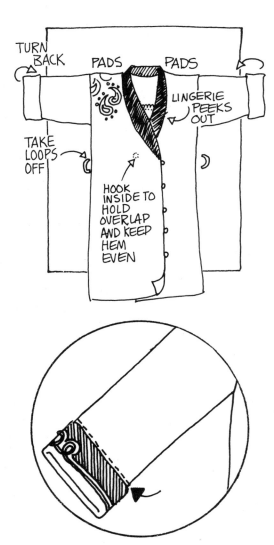

TURN BACK

PADS   PADS

LINGERIE PEEKS OUT

TAKE LOOPS OFF

HOOK INSIDE TO HOLD OVERLAP AND KEEP HEM EVEN

SHORTEN A FANCY SLEEVE BY TAKING A TUCK ALONG THE CUFF LINE. TURN IT INSIDE-OUT AND SEW.

Turn a smoking jacket into a dress by adding buttons. To shorten a fancy sleeve, take a tuck as illustrated.

THE LUXE OF ANTIQUE SMOKING JACKETS

Here's another look that makes you feel very "dressed" and is also extremely comfortable and easy to wear. It begins with a man's antique smoking jacket, which is essentially a robe made in elegant paisley fabric with satin shawl collar and cuffs. (You've seen them often in Noël Coward plays.) Find them at thrift shops. Wear a smoking jacket over a tuxedo shirt, on which you've sewn crystal buttons instead of the standard-issue white ones, with silk pajama pants or tuxedo pants held up with suspenders (no one sees these—they're under the shirt). Sash the robe low around the hips and under the tummy. Because of

Rx for a Sit-Down Dinner

A cocktail party, where you have to stand up for several hours, is not much fun for a pregnant woman. But a dinner party at which you spend hours sitting on a hard wooden chair is not much better.

After one particular night spent in great discomfort, I decided to plan for my comfort in the future. I chose a pretty cushion in the shape of a heart and sewed a satin ribbon on it as a shoulder strap. Whenever I was invited out and was unsure of what the seating arrangements might be, I slung the cushion over my shoulder like an evening bag and knew I'd spend the night in seated bliss.

the large size you'll need in order to have the robe wrap sufficiently in front, the sleeves and shoulders may be big and slightly out of kilter. To alter the sleeves without hiding a handsome cuff, simply take a tuck above the cuff. As for the shoulders, bolder ones look best, anyway, so don't change a thing. Just support the extra width with shoulder pads. Or, if you prefer, let the shoulder drape softly. It's a robe, after all, and doesn't need to look strictly tailored.

Using the same robe, you can create a rich, romantic coatdress you'll be able to wear almost anywhere. To keep the robe securely closed, add a hook inside and use buttons (creating fabric loops on one side instead of buttonholes), as shown at left. Or attach a vertical line of Velcro in front. Buy the stick-on kind so you can move it as you get bigger. Undoubtedly you'll also have to put in a fairly substantial hem. Maintain the period mood with a lace camisole or a lace scarf at the neck and lace stockings.

GLITZY SWEATERS

A luxurious evening sweater romanced with rhinestone buttons doesn't sound like something you'd invest in now, does it? But think about it. An evening sweater is just a regular sweater with fancy buttons.

All you need to make an inexpensive version is an oversized cardigan in a suitably rich-colored knit. Lots of men's sweaters fill the bill, including golf sweaters. (You can place a pin or appliqué over any insignia.) Of course, check thrift shops before buying new. Once you've chosen the sweater, snip off the buttons and sew on the glitziest new ones you can find. A silky camisole worn underneath will keep you covered.

Hairstyles to Add Pizzazz

Keeping the focus on your face rather than your figure is one of the basics you should always have in mind. And what better way to achieve that than with a fabulous "do" for evening? The possibilities are limitless, but here are a few suggestions to get those creative juices flowing.

MOUSSED "CAP" EAR TO EAR

FRIZZ THE REST

EVENING

LONG HAIR CASUALLY LOOPED AROUND FABRIC MAKES A CHIGNON ON TOP

SLICK YOUR BOB WITH GEL FOR SHINE

For bottoms you can use the pants from a set of men's silk pajamas or a tube skirt or any matching wool skirt. Or pick up a pair of satin maternity pants.

A HALTER TOP AND WRAP SKIRT

A bare and graceful no-sew halter top and wrap skirt require very little besides body confidence. They can be formal or casual, depending on fabric and accessories.

You'll need two rectangular pieces of fabric—one for the skirt and one for the top. Cotton knit or silk or polyester jersey are what I recommend, since they don't even have to be hemmed. The skirt should be twice your hip or stomach size (whichever is larger) and at least 45 inches wide. The top should measure your chest size plus 36 inches.

I think the effect is sleekest, and dressiest, in black. But it can be beautiful, too, in white, beige, or any jewel tone.

To put on the halter top, wrap the smaller square around you as you would a

---

WRAP ON A HALTER TOP AND SKIRT

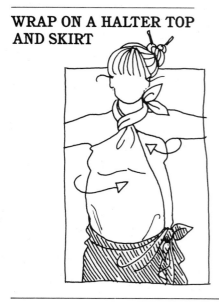

A Leisurely Bath

———

Before you go out, make time for a leisurely bath, applying new makeup, and splashing on a wonderful fragrance. During pregnancy, you naturally feel warmer and perspire more, so freshening up is especially important to put you in a festive mood.

I asked Catherine Kanner, who wrote and illustrated the exquisite *Book of the Bath*, to create a bath recipe especially for pregnant women. Here is her answer:

GENTLE ROSE AND CUCUMBER BATH

A relaxing and refreshing bath that can be taken anytime.

1 cucumber
½ cup rose petals (fresh or dried)
1 cup water

Peel and slice the cucumber and place in a bowl. Boil the water and pour over the cucumber slices. Let stand until the cucumber becomes mushy, then strain. Steep rose petals in the remaining juice for one hour (or longer). Strain again and add the fragrant juice to warm bath water. Bathe to your body's delight.

towel, ending up with the two ends in front. Cross one end over the other, as shown below left, and tie them behind your neck.

To put on the skirt, wrap the larger square around your hips, under your tummy, and over the halter top. Knot it on one hip, letting the rest fall open on your leg. (Pin it together below the knot if you're modest.) Wear a pair of colored, but sheer, hose to lessen the contrast between leg and skirt and add ankle-strap sandals. Get ready to enjoy the attention!

Making the Clothes You Have Feel Sexy

Often all you need to put on the ritz is a new way of wearing an old standby. Try these sensual moves with clothes you already own:

• Stretch the neckline of a boat-necked top to expose one bare shoulder.

• Try wearing a jacket without a top for a change. Hold the jacket together at the cleavage with a brooch. Wear a few fine chains or a choker of velvet ribbon around your neck.

• Do you own a longish skirt with a drawstring waist? Pull it up above your waist and wear it as a strapless dress.

• Dye a pair of long underwear black, then float a diaphanous piece of hemmed black silk chiffon on top. If you're not that bold, make it a piece of opaque silk.

• Dancers gather their leotards in front to draw more attention to their busts. Use the same technique, as illustrated, on your knit tanks, tops, and sweaters, using a decorative pin.

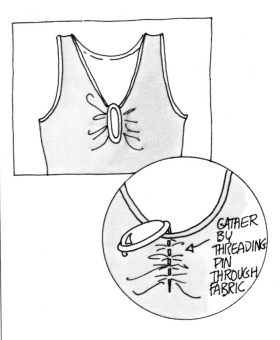

GATHER BY THREADING PIN THROUGH FABRIC

• A narrow knit skirt worn with sheer hose and pumps will add sex appeal to just about any top.

• Add inexpensive but glitzy accessories to your present wardrobe. Have fun choosing stockings, for example. Sheer black ones are particularly sexy, and anything with a pattern is pretty. Consider trying a garter belt. Not only is it sexy, but it's practical, since you can wear it under your belly. If you've never worn one before, now you've got a wonderful excuse! Lacy gloves, a flirty hat, a ribbon in your hair, or a linen handkerchief can also transform a boring outfit into a knockout. (See Chapter 8 for more on accessories.)

These ideas for party wear—and the new ones they spark in your mind—should carry you through nine months of glamorous evenings. Enjoy!

CHAPTER 6

Sports Style

It's certainly possible to make it through your pregnancy wearing nothing more on the weekends than maternity jeans and casual tops. But before you settle into such a conventional free-time uniform, take a look at some of the creative ideas presented by women in my survey. These and others in this chapter should convince you that chic doesn't have to stop when you ease out of your pumps.

Free-Time Favorites

When it came to weekend clothes, stylist Marilise Flusser said, "My aim was to look happy, fun, and energetic. If I felt tired, I just washed my hair and put on a great outfit! My favorite was a Mickey Mouse T-shirt over a Norma Kamali double-ruffle miniskirt with an elasticized waist, sneakers, and funny socks. And shoulder pads—always." Model Yasmine loved wearing enormous leather overalls—surplus from the Swedish airforce—which she picked up at Canal Jeans in New York. Underneath she wore a skinny top: "The contrast between the big bottom and the little top was incredibly sexy—so my hus-

band said, anyway."

Ingrid Alpert, a model, and wife of shoe designer Marc Alpert, felt best in bright colors. In her fifth month, she told me, "I just bought a fuchsia shirt and orange leggings. When I'm pregnant, I love wearing bright, happy shades." And Kate Castelbajac, wife of designer Jean-Charles, lived in the big white shirts she unearthed at Parisian flea markets, teamed with drawstring pants.

Menswear comes in especially handy for building a free-time pregnancy wardrobe. You can find just about everything you need in the way of tops, pants, sweaters, and jackets in your husband's closet or in a thrift shop—the sizes will be right, the styles classic, and the prices reasonable. All the clothes require are a little feminizing and tailoring to suit your personality and figure. Look back at Chapter 3 for lots of ideas on raiding a man's wardrobe.

THE LEAN LOOK OF LEGGINGS

The look I heard touted again and again for leisure-time wear was leggings worn with a big shirt. It's perfectly suited to and incredibly flattering for pregnant bodies. It's also as appropriate for a woman who's five feet tall as for one who is much taller. Many maternity-clothing manufacturers have come out with leggings (basically thick tights without feet), but you can probably find a pair more cheaply in regular hosiery departments. Just go for a size or two larger than your usual.

Magazine editor Judsen Culbreth adopted the shirt-and-leggings look early on in her pregnancy and felt that it was slimming from the first day to the last. One actress bought several black and white shirts and leggings, mixing and matching them to change the looks. Black and white is crisp—and very far away from the usual "dolly" effect. With just four pieces, she was able to create a number of very different outfits. It was a simple, economical— and great-looking—approach.

Five-foot-two-inch publicist Alyssa Rabach Anthone also loved leggings. She wore hers with men's sweaters instead of shirts, adding shoulder pads for balance. Because she is so petite, Alyssa felt that matching the sweater and leggings for a one-color, one-line look was especially flattering. Experiment with your own combinations, perhaps layering big shirts with sweaters or vests and longish jackets. Comfort and a great look will be your rewards.

JUMP INTO JUMPSUITS

The long line and easy fit of a square-cut, no-waist jumpsuit can solve many weekend wardrobe dilemmas when you're pregnant. During the first few months, wear them with belts, and then gradually belt them more and more loosely until you finally remove the belt altogether. Then belt them up again as your figure returns to normal after the birth. As one woman found, "Because I really liked the styles, I was happy to wear them after the baby was born, too. Within a few days I could start wearing the belts again, which made me feel normal quicker, instead of trying to get into my regular clothes, which would only have been frustrating and uncomfortable." Try the jumpsuits worn by mechanics or airline workers, which you can find at army/navy or uniform stores. (See Chapter 3.) Or just check the department stores—jumpsuits seem never to go out of style. Always try them on to be sure of a comfortable, roomy fit you can grow in.

THE BIKINI ROMPER

A hot-weather look I loved was a romper made from a man's shirt and a pair of men's bikini underwear (without the pocket). As I've said elsewhere, the underwear is more comfortable than women's.

Relax and cool off in a romper fashioned from a man's shirt and his bikini underwear.

Warm-Weather Options

These variations on the bikini romper (instructions are on page 92) can help you beat the heat. The basis of each is a pair of men's cotton bikini underwear (without the pocket), which is wonderfully comfortable for pregnant bodies. If your legs feel too bare, tie on fabric as a skirt.

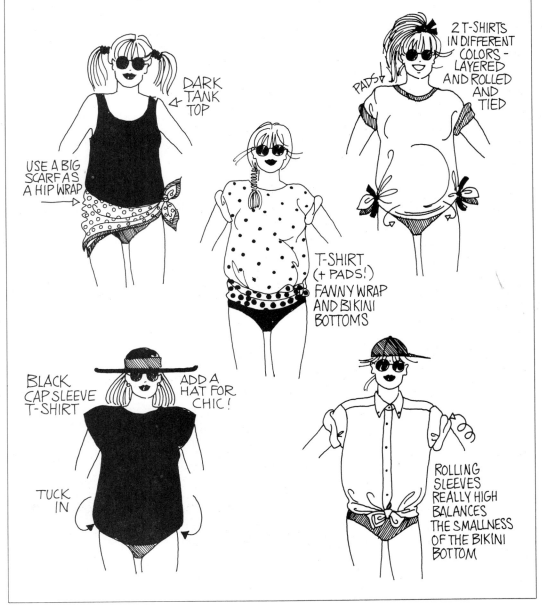

DARK TANK TOP

USE A BIG SCARF AS A HIP WRAP

2 T-SHIRTS IN DIFFERENT COLORS – LAYERED AND ROLLED AND TIED

PADS

T-SHIRT (+ PADS!) FANNY WRAP AND BIKINI BOTTOMS

BLACK CAP SLEEVE T-SHIRT

ADD A HAT FOR CHIC!

TUCK IN

ROLLING SLEEVES REALLY HIGH BALANCES THE SMALLNESS OF THE BIKINI BOTTOM

Try to get hold of an extra-large shirt so there's plenty of fabric to work with. To begin, pull on the bikini bottoms, then button the shirt down to the shirttails (don't forget your shoulder pads). Tie the tails, letting the shirt blouse over your tummy. Last, roll the sleeves up to your most flattering length. You can also make rompers with T-shirts or tank tops, as illustrated on page 91. If a romper's barer than you can wear, buy a couple of yards of fabric and tie it over the shirt at the hip, for an instant skirt.

Dressing for Action

I confess, I didn't exercise a lot when I was pregnant. Formal toe-touch and push-up kinds of exercises are just not my cup of tea—pregnant or not. I did swim. And I did play tennis. Now and then. The most regular form of exercise I did was walking. Just down the road from where I live there is a wildlife preserve where I often took long walks to get away from it all. During my second pregnancy, my walks frequently turned into runs, though not out of choice: I had to run to keep up with Lindsay, my then-toddler son.

The survey I conducted before writing this book showed me a very different picture of pregnancy and exercise. Lackadaisical exercisers like myself, I found, are in the minority. Far more common are women who make a point of regular workouts—squeezing in classes during lunchtime, or before or after work. The word I got was that exercise made them not more exhausted, but actually more relaxed.

As important as you may believe exercise to be, it's tempting to skimp on appro-

priate clothes. After all, nobody important is going to be watching while you work out (important meaning anyone from the office). True...but there's more to it than that. Studies have shown that the clothes you wear affect your mood and your performance at play as well as at work. Think about taking a ballet class in ratty old sweatpants and a wrinkled T-shirt. Would you feel as graceful or as confident as you would dressed in a sleek black leotard and pale-pink tights? Doubtful. But don't worry—you can look and feel good while you exercise, and still pinch pennies. Here are a few ways to do it.

AT EXERCISE CLASS

The preferred type of exercise for many women I surveyed was an exercise class—either at a Y or health club, or at home with a videotape or record. A marketing manager remarked, "Exercise was very important to both my physical and mental health. I think your body tells you what is best for you. I did have to cut back some toward the end. I just changed my routine to more gentle stretching and breathing." And a corporate lawyer who found it difficult to attend regularly scheduled classes found an exercise video endorsed by the American College of Obstetricians and Gynecologists. "To my surprise, I kept to a very consistent schedule, exercising to the tape at least three times a week because I enjoyed it so much. I really worked out a lot of soreness and tension."

Once you've found a class or video—or record or tape—that suits your needs, you have to settle on something to wear during exercise that will keep you comfortable and confident. If you have a plain stretch leotard—not the new, shiny lycra kind, which are too much like girdles—you'll probably find that you can wear it comfortably quite far into your pregnancy. At some point, you may want to buy one a size or two larger. Since you want to keep your investment low, look for classic black leotards at discount stores, where they often stock off-brands for a lot less. Check, too, for famous-brand irregulars at very reduced prices.

In tights, look for queen-sized versions of your favorites. Footless tights are a good idea now, because you can move them up your leg as your tummy takes more fabric at the top. Wear a pair of socks and leg warmers to cover what the tights don't.

One woman I interviewed found that after a certain point, tights no longer felt comfortable. She switched to looser sweatpants for comfort. Dancer Patricia Davant continued to wear her billowy, parachute-fabric warm-up suit to prenatal exercise classes with a cotton leotard underneath. "People were always commenting on how great it looked." Just make sure the fabric you wear during exercise doesn't make you overheat. Magazine editor Janet Chan felt great wearing her husband Tyler's old gym shorts and polo shirts. Model Yasmine boldly wore unitards. "They were in a cotton blend that stretched to fit, even though I gained over 70 pounds!"

For comfort, it's hard to beat a man's extra large T-shirt over white or black tights and leotard. It's neat, cheap, and good-looking. Why spend more? If you want to deemphasize the tent look, slit the T about five inches up from the center bottom and tie the cut ends together to cradle your tummy. Or pull the bottom of the T-shirt to one side, roll the extra material, and tie it in a knot, as illustrated.

Boxer shorts and a T-shirt are roomy and comfortable—perfect for exercising.

EXERCISE IN STYLE

3–6 MONTHS

TERRY SWEAT BANDS IN LOTS OF COLORS

TIE THE T-SHIRT AT THE HIP

LEG WARMERS ADD COLOR.

6–8 MONTHS

LAYER CUT OFF T-SHIRTS

ADDING LOTS OF FUN COLORS

Wear big T-shirts over large leotards and tights. Tie the shirt or cut it off, depending on your size.

They come three per package, so you will always have a spare, clean and ready to pack in your exercise bag. If you made any of the adapted T-shirts from Chapter 2, wear them now.

As you grow, just buy bigger shirts. Cut and layer them as shown on page 93, adding interest above what used to be your waist. Try a man's red T-shirt under a big yellow tank. Or pale blue under pale green. Or purple under kelly green. If your local men's department is short on colors, check out a jeans store or your town's army/navy store. All of the tops you're buying now will more than pay for themselves after the baby is born. An abundant supply of easy-to-launder T-shirts can be a new mom's best friend.

ON THE COURT

Most doctors say tennis is fine during pregnancy, especially during the early months, so there is no reason for seasoned players to take to the sidelines. (If you've never played before, however, now is not the time to begin.) Do check with your doctor first and take some extra care—avoid overlong matches and trying for balls that make you stretch too far. Make sure you've got your balance and try not to get overheated.

When it comes to your tennis wardrobe, white is always right. I loved wearing a big white smock of a dress (bought one size larger than my usual in a non-maternity department), tied at the hips with a sash. As you can see in the photo at right, the dress had few details, which made it easy to alter with accessories for a whole range of less active occasions. For tennis, I wore it with white socks and sneakers, and it was perfect.

You can also look for antique white

A white smock dress and hip sash make the perfect match on the court.

cotton slips to wear as tennis dresses. If the one you find is too bare on top, slip a white T-shirt on underneath. Hike the skirt up with a hip sash to above-the-knee length to keep the fabric out of the way of play.

Men's tennis shorts are perfect for you at this time. Wear a white T-shirt or polo shirt and use a pair of white suspenders on top to keep everything together. Roll a colorful cotton bandanna and tie it around your neck for a natty finish. Here's a tip: Tuck the shirt into your underwear to keep it in place.

Safety First

I n response to the huge number of exercise regimens being marketed to pregnant women, the American College of Obstetricians and Gynecologists has issued the following exercise guidelines designed to protect the health of the baby. Pregnant women should:

- Drink plenty of fluids before, after, and, if necessary, during exercise.

- Avoid exercise during hot, humid weather or when feverish.

- Keep their heart rates lower than 140 beats per minute.

- Avoid any exercise that is performed lying on the back after the completion of the fourth month.

- Avoid jerky, bouncy movements as well as either deep flexion or full extension of the joints.

- Include five-minute warm-up and cool-down periods in exercise routines.

- Exercise regularly—at least three times a week—rather than sporadically.

- Avoid any strenuous activity that lasts over 15 minutes.

- Be alert to any unusual symptoms. Stop exercising immediately if they occur, and call the doctor.

ON THE SLOPES AND TRAILS

Although you should resist any urges to break Olympic ski records or climb Mount Everest, you can still enjoy some hiking and skiing while you're pregnant. (Again, check with your doctor to be sure.) Some doctors recommend switching to cross-country skiing during pregnancy because it's generally considered a much safer sport than downhill skiing. Watch yourself in any case—be careful not to get too cold or overheated. Be sensible enough to stop and rest when you are tired.

In the early months, when you can still ski but can't fit into your regular ski clothes, keep warm by piling on layers. Start with long underwear—a couple of pairs if it's cold enough—topped by a man's pullover or sweatshirt, and men's ski pants held up with suspenders. If you can't find an extra pair of men's pants to borrow, pull on a pair of overalls.

Overalls are a good choice for hiking, too. They don't bind and the fabric's strong, protective, and absorbent. Put on several tops underneath for warmth, peeling them off as needed. Be sure to wear a good support or sport bra—cotton is good because it's firm and absorbent. Take care not to get overheated. Bring along a canteen and take frequent swallows to replace lost fluids. Pack a damp washcloth and press it to your forehead and the back of your neck at regular intervals to cool off. Invest in a good, supportive shoe and absorbent socks in cotton or wool.

IN THE SWIM

Swimming was high on the list of favorite forms of exercise among respondents to my questionnaires. What many liked most was feeling almost weightless at a time when they were particularly loaded down. As one teacher reported, "I don't usually enjoy swimming all that much. I'm more into

Sun and Pregnancy

Pregnancy stimulates melanin production, which makes tanning extra easy during this time. The problem comes in getting more than you bargained for in terms of chloasma (mask of pregnancy) and other skin discolorations. Dale Abadir, a dermatologist, recommends keeping your skin shielded from the sun as much as possible, especially the extrasensitive areas, like your face. This means using protective clothing—cover-ups and wide-brimmed hats—as well as lotions. Dr. Abadir warns that even sunscreens with SPFs of 15 or more will not completely protect your skin. She recommends using one of the new sunscreens that completely block the tanning ultraviolet rays. If you notice areas darkening, you may ask your dermatologist or doctor to recommend a cream or gel containing hydroquinone, which will help to lighten the discolorations. The safest route to a healthy glow? Dr. Abadir suggests using a tan accelerator, which gives skin convincing color without sun exposure. The idea is to apply it a couple of hours before heading out into the sun. Then add a heavy-duty sunscreen when you go outside.

Nautilus and working out with weights. But after my seventh month, I tried swimming and stuck with it until I delivered. I loved the buoyancy of it. It literally gets the weight off your feet." Another woman started swimming earlier on. "Swimming saved me in the early months when I was so tired I had trouble making it through the workday. There was a pool in a building right next to where my office was. Three times a week, during lunch, I went and swam laps. I came back feeling relaxed, exercised, and more energetic."

When it came to clothes for sports, the single biggest complaint from my questionnaire respondents was on the subject of bathing suits. Comments on maternity suits ranged from "horrible-looking," "matronly," "old-fashioned," and "too expensive" to "I took one look at what was available and decided to skip the beach that summer." Some women found they could get away with wearing their old tank-style suits up until the very last months. Some turned to stretchy dance leotards, buying them one size larger than usual and wearing them with bras.

What I did was simply put off making a decision altogether and continue wearing bikinis as usual. Until Hawaii....It was the first morning of a one-week vacation and I was four months pregnant. Blithely, I climbed into my bikini. It felt tighter than usual, so I walked over to the mirror to size up the situation. One look was all it took. There was no way I was going out on the beach like that! But I certainly wasn't going to miss out on the sun, the beach, and the water. I began looking around my hotel room for an answer. The first thing I found that had potential was a pair of my husband's stretch bikini underwear. The second was a pareo, that I had previously used as a cover-up.

This cool and comfortable swimsuit is easy to tie on. For instructions and variations, see pages 98 and 99.

Necessity—and the traumatic thought of trying on maternity suits under harsh dressing-room lights—really does spur invention. The suit I came up with that morning (see photo above) became a staple in my maternity wardrobe, and in the wardrobes of many of my friends. I like the look so much that I wear it even now. As a maternity bathing suit, it's hard to top.

A double layer of fabric in front keeps you modest and gracefully covers such pregnancy-related body changes as bulging belly buttons and expanding breasts. If your weight gain has made you self-conscious, you can use a second pareo as a skirt at the hips. Wear it to the edge of the water, then slip it off. Take a dip, then knot

Quick, Easy, After-Exercise Makeup

Always start exercise with clean skin. You don't want moisturizer or makeup to clog sweat ducts, possibly setting off a rash. Afterward, when you're rosy, glowing, and fresh from exercise and a shower, take advantage of it—keep makeup to a minimum.

- Use a sheer foundation, blended well, just where you need it— around your nose and on your chin and forehead. Keep it light, sheer. Cover up under-eye circles with a concealer, if necessary.

- Complement the cheek color you've already got with a gel blush. It's the most natural-looking type, best on damp skin.

- Skip eye shadow. Instead, curl lashes and apply mascara.

- Stay away from harsh red lip color. Go for soft, pretty shades of pale pink, peach, or mauve.

it back on as soon as you emerge. What could be easier? And the slit that opens as you walk is very sexy. Last—but definitely not least—is the unbeatable price. If you've got a pair of bikini bottoms to borrow and a length of fabric, as I did, the suit will cost you nothing. If not, you can certainly put one together for under ten dollars. At that price, you can afford several.

Tie on a Perfect Swimsuit

Many women find the swimsuits in maternity departments less than flattering. An easy alternative is the wrap-style suit, which can be tied on several ways. You might choose a bright Tahitian print for one, a sophisticated solid black for another, a feminine Laura Ashley print for a third. Here's how to wrap yours up:

- Pull on a pair of cotton men's bikini briefs (without the pocket).

- Wrap a length of fabric two times your bust measurement and wide enough to reach from shoulder to hip around you as if you're drying your back with a towel. Tie the two top ends in a knot just above your bust.

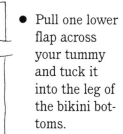

- Pull one lower flap across your tummy and tuck it into the leg of the bikini bottoms.

- Pull the second flap across the same way and tuck into the other leg. The legs of the bikinis keep the fabric firmly tucked.

- Adjust the fullness.

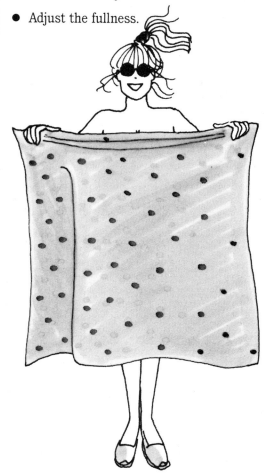

For variety, here is another way to tie one on:

- Using the same pareo, hold it lengthwise this time against your body in front.

- Bring the top two corners above your bust, under your arms, and around to the back and knot. Now, pull the rest of the fabric through your legs, diaper-style.

TWIST ENDS, BRING AROUND FRONT AND TIE

- Holding the bottom two ends, bring them back to the front and tie them under your tummy.

TIE ENDS IN FRONT

To add a skirt:

- Wrap another length of fabric, twice your hip measurement, as a skirt around your hips and under your tummy. Tie at the side.

- If you're not going to be swimming, top the pareo skirt with a crisp man's white shirt or T-shirt.

Now that you've saved a fortune on a suit, don't blow your budget on a cover-up. Here's how to save without sacrificing good looks. Try:

• A white or dyed lab coat

• A man's white shirt

• A Japanese kimono

• A caftan cut to knee length

• An extra-large, extra-long man's T-shirt

• A man's Hawaiian shirt

• A cozy terry-cloth poncho that does double duty as a beach towel. Make it easily out of a large towel, following the instructions for the poncho given on page 110.

For the Spectator

If your taste in sports runs to football and basketball and baseball, pregnancy may be the time to explore the pleasures of being a spectator. Here are some ways to be a fan worth watching.

Try this great look for watching a baseball game. For comfort, spiff up a man's white shirt with a bolo tie, teamed with a denim jacket and a pair of drawstring pants rolled up to just under your knees. Roll socks down to the top of your sneakers.

At football games, the problem is often cold weather. One respondent to my questionnaire had season tickets to see the Buffalo Bills. Buffalo is really, really cold, so she had a lot of warming up to do. Her solution was to start with a pair of long underwear. Since she was quite big at the time, she needed to sew a maternity panel into the front of the underwear bottoms.

Thirsty? Carry a Canteen

One day I was thumbing through a magazine and an ad caught my eye, though not for any of the usual reasons. The model was wearing a canteen. It suddenly struck me that a canteen would be the perfect thing to carry around with me. After all, wasn't I always thirsty? Didn't I always find myself miles away from a soda machine or snack bar? So I headed over to my local sports shop and picked one up. I couldn't leave well enough alone, so I cut off the strap and tied on a ribbon. Better already, I thought. I took to filling up the canteen with ice water before I went out, slinging it over my shoulder, and taking swigs all day. With its cheery ribbon strap, it actually worked as an accessory, too.

Then she put on two shirts—a man's white shirt under a red-and-black flannel one. She pulled the collar of the white shirt out over the top of the flannel one and rolled the white sleeves over the flannel. On top of all that went a pair of men's overalls, wool socks, and ankle boots. Finally, she put on her husband's duffle coat. The effect was very neat and pulled together, and she stayed warm to boot.

For watching tennis matches, a favorite look of mine was a white tube skirt with a man's white shirt tied under the tummy, white socks, and classic white tennis shoes. Or go a more romantic route with a pure white caftan. It's a wonderful choice if you need a feminine lift. Wear it with white strappy sandals or leather pumps and silver jewelry.

For fun and protection from the sun, take a cotton scarf—the more colorful the better—and place it on your head, one edge resting on the crown, the rest sailing behind. Then anchor it in place by putting a baseball cap or visor on top.

WHAT TO PACK IN YOUR BACKPACK

Now that backpacks come in the most wonderful range of colors and fabrics, there's no reason in the world not to take advantage of them. They are so practical, comfortable, and sensible for pregnant women on the go—a perfect way to tote all you need to take anywhere when you'll need supplies but want your hands free.

Here's a list of items to pack for the ball game:

- A cushion. You'll use it to sit on during the game or to set down under a tree and take five if the game goes into extra innings. You can also place it under your knees to relieve pressure on your back. Indispensable!

- A tablecloth, pareo, or blanket—something clean and soft for you to lay down on or settle over your shoulders if the day or night turns cool.

- A clean washcloth soaked in water and packed in a plastic bag. Place it on your face or neck if you feel hot.

- Sunglasses, sunscreen, and lip balm.

- Fruit juices in portable cartons.

- Moist towelettes for sticky fingers.

From wide-brimmed hat and waterproof jacket to backpack, canteen, and pillow, this outfit combines being prepared with looking great for a day at the ballpark.

- Crackers, fruit, or other favorite snacks. Pregnant women are always hungry, and you won't want to be forced into eating hot dogs when hunger hits.

- Travel packs of astringent—in little foil envelopes—to refresh and cool your skin.

- Tissues.

- Hair brush and comb. Add a scarf or elastic bands for hair repairs. A hat works well, too, and it keeps the sun from your head and eyes.

- Toothbrush and toothpaste.

Whether you're working out, hiking, playing tennis, swimming—or just watching and cheering others on—dress for the occasion and you'll enjoy it even more. Go for comfort and a sense of fun, taking advantage of your temporary condition as a reason to be unique.

CHAPTER 7

Braving the Elements

As winter approaches and the thermometer begins its descent, you gingerly try on last year's wool coat, hoping against hope that it'll see you through the cold months—somehow. But what do you do if the buttons refuse to meet the buttonholes? You can't go through the coldest months of the year with your coat flying open (though I have seen some pregnant women do just that). The point of this chapter is to show that you can keep warm and dry and look great without blowing your budget. Here is a whole range of economical keep-warm options for work, weekend, and evening.

Men's Coats

As I've hinted before, my penchant for raiding men's departments didn't stop with suits and sports clothes. It extended to outerwear as well. I happen to think men's trench coats look terrific on women. The shoulders are nice and wide, which is espe-

cially flattering for pregnancy, and the folds fall quite gracefully. If your husband happens to own an extra trench with a zip-out lining, you're set for all seasons. Just add shoulder pads, roll up the sleeves, and tie the belt rakishly in the back.

One Brooklyn lawyer and mother of three wore her husband's Brooks Brothers single-breasted wool overcoat to work, tucking a silk scarf in the collar for a feminine touch. On weekends she dipped into his closet again, choosing a down jacket that she wore with corduroy pants.

Check those thrift-store racks for men's overcoats in classic fabrics and styles. These large items are some of the best secondhand buys around, costing a mere fraction of what a new woman's coat goes for these days. A teacher from Buffalo, New York—where cold is a serious fact of life—found an old tweed man's coat at her neighborhood thrift shop. It was the very traditional kind with a high collar and hidden buttons. To inject some style, she added shoulder pads and tied a secondhand fox scarf at the neck. Instant class!

Obviously, you should choose a man's

Coat Make-Overs

Before you rush out to buy a new coat, take a careful look at those you've already got in your closet. If there is any possibility of altering them, it's certainly worth a try.

- An old wrap-style coat—the kind with no buttons and a self-belt, like a robe—can expand easily. Leave the belt off and use a decorative button for closure. Or tack on ties, a hook and eye, or strips of Velcro. You might even get away with simply holding the coat closed with your shoulder bag, as shown.

- To really dress up an old wrap coat, add fur trim to collar and cuffs.

- Like the double-breasted suit jackets discussed in Chapter 4, double-breasted wool or trench coats are naturals to redo for pregnancy. All you have to do is move some buttons to turn them into roomy single-breasted coats. (See page 62 for how-tos.)

- Take a look at men's casual wraps. Tweed jackets, down vests over bulky sweaters, red-and-black-checked lumber jackets, and hunting jackets can all be pressed into weekend service. For cool-but-not-cold days, borrow (or buy second-hand) a man's heavyweight cardigan and dress it up with fur trim, as illustrated. Don't forget those shoulder pads!

LET YOUR SHOULDER BAG HOLD YOUR COAT CLOSED - IF YOU CAN'T CLOSE IT ANYMORE

TIES

TIGHT CUFFS KEEP YOU WARM

ADD FUR TRIM TO YOUR WRAP COAT - ADD A BUTTON TO HOLD AT THE SIDE

PADS

ADD A FUR COLLAR AND CUFFS TO A MAN'S SWEATER

coat that is large but not overwhelming. Check length as well as width—it's probably not worth buying a secondhand coat that you'll have to have hemmed or otherwise professionally altered. Add control widthwise by buckling a belt under the bust, empire style, or around the hips, under your belly. Use a fairly wide leather belt for the best proportion.

Buying for Now... and Later

It may be that—because your pregnancy will stretch through the whole winter, or because you're not comfortable in a man's coat—you decide to take the plunge and purchase a new coat. If that's the case, just be sure to take your time and shop until you find a coat you really love, one that you won't stash away in mothballs after one season of wear.

Fortunately, in recent years there's been a large supply of the kind of big, roomy, swingy coats a pregnant woman can feel right at home in. The big-coat trend seems to be due in part to the professional woman's need for a wrap that can comfortably accommodate a suit jacket underneath. The result is that a pregnant woman who needs a new coat can take her pick from regular sizes, confident that the coat will serve her well for years to come.

FULL-LENGTH CLOTH COATS

Color and style are the two most important factors in insuring that your investment in an everyday coat pays off. A good black

A man's trench coat is roomy yet stylish—perfect for pregnant figures. Tie the belt under your tummy.

coat will easily take you from day to evening and will coordinate with all the colors in your wardrobe. Rich brown or navy are the second-best choices. Take into account the colors that predominate in your closet. As for style, if your aim is to buy a coat that'll take you through several seasons, look for classic shapes without a lot of trendy details, which may be dated before long. And, of course, look for a roomy shape—raglan or drop-shoulder, beltless or with a removable belt. With their shawl collars, extra fabric in front, and straight lines, wrap coats are a very good choice. Use the ideas on the opposite page to make them grow with you.

During my first pregnancy, I bought a very unconstructed chocolate-brown sheepskin coat with a stand-up collar and full sleeves. Nine years—and one more pregnancy—later, I'm still enjoying it. The coat's simple style seems to endow it with a chameleon-like quality. It looks as right at night as it does dressed down for the country with work boots and a raccoon fling. That coat was certainly money well spent.

Corporate lawyer Madeline Kuflik was similarly fortunate. When she was just two months pregnant, she bought a Calvin Klein coat that was cut big from the bust down and came with a detachable belt. She wore it belted as long as she could, then put the belt away in a drawer, allowing the coat to drape softly around her. Since she had already seen how the coat looked early in her pregnancy, she knew she would like the way it looked *sans* baby—and enjoyed wearing it the next year. That's important when you're making such a big investment.

To help you make the important outerwear decision, here's a rundown of some other great nonmaternity styles to use through your ninth month and beyond.

QUILTED COATS AND JACKETS

Whether filled with down or with polyester Fiberfil, these coats signal guaranteed warmth and, quite often for pregnant women, guaranteed fit as well. According to my survey, women had more luck getting their quilted coats to close over full-term bellies than any other kind. Most quilted coats have another plus. They can be thrown in the washing machine, significantly reducing your dry-cleaning bill.

If you're buying your coat new for pregnancy, look for one with vertical stitching, simple lines, and a stand-up col-

lar. All are details that help streamline the coat. Snap or knit cuffs are nice to have to prevent cold air from rushing in. Stay away from such bulk-adders as puffy pockets, big lapels, horizontal seaming, and cuffed sleeves.

If you're making do with a quilted jacket you (or your husband) already own, it may need some extending in the late months. Try tying a long wool scarf across

COVER THE GAP

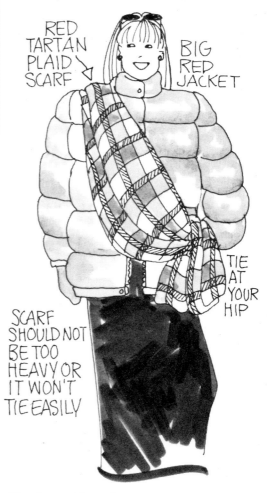

RED TARTAN PLAID SCARF

BIG RED JACKET

TIE AT YOUR HIP

SCARF SHOULD NOT BE TOO HEAVY OR IT WON'T TIE EASILY

Tie a long wool scarf across your quilted jacket if you can't zip it up.

your body, as shown, to cover the gap. Keep the gap as small as possible by tacking on ties. (Some down jackets come with drawstrings at the waist. If yours does, just replace the usually short string with a longer one to hold the front closed.)

For weekends, you might enjoy the style and warmth of a down vest. When you shop, look for long vests that reach to the tops of your thighs, for the neatest look.

CAPES

Instantly adaptable to pregnant bodies, capes are a great cold-weather solution, but it makes sense to buy one only if you really enjoy wearing them. Some women find the restricted arm movement annoying. Others don't seem to mind it. Capes do make it difficult to carry a shoulder bag, for instance. Attaché cases, though, don't present a problem. If you're not sure about capes, borrow one before you buy. Wear it a few times and see if you feel comfortable. In its favor, a cape creates a classic silhouette that never goes out of style. The lines are soft, flowing, and quite flattering to all figure types.

One Detroit banker I talked to had her long-range strategy well planned when she purchased a long red cape early in her pregnancy. Her idea was to make the cape her primary coat while she was pregnant, wearing it both day and evening. Then, the following year, she intended to buy a more traditional coat for day, keeping the cape for special nights. That way, she felt, the purchase was justified.

Beatrice Breguet, president of her own public relations firm in Paris, is a committed cape wearer who felt that her black cape gave her both the sophistication and authority she needed while pregnant. College professor Marsha Stein made herself a cape using a Halston pattern. She was surprised to find that she continued to wear it for years afterward. Australian *Vogue* editor Nancy Pilcher, possibly the busiest person I know, always looked perfect zooming around in her black cape. Two pregnancies later, it's still hanging in her closet and worn often.

In shopping for a cape, choose one with simple, clean lines in a classic, dark color. The cape should fall below your knees and be roomy enough to last through your pregnancy. Don't neglect to check thrift shops, since capes tend to go in and out of fashion and may have been discarded in very good condition. Accessorize with matching—or strongly contrasting—gloves, bracelets, high boots, or hose.

BLOUSON JACKETS

If you find yourself wishing for some variety in your outerwear, a blouson jacket is one purchase that makes perfect sense. With their generously cut torsos and tight hips, blouson jackets genuinely complement—and easily fit—pregnant bodies.

I have a black blouson jacket in a very soft leather that I loved wearing when I was pregnant. At the beginning, I wore the jacket whenever I didn't want my pregnancy to become an issue. It seemed to quell suspicions because its blousiness provided a perfect camouflage for those few extra inches. It continued to serve me well right through my sixth month.

Blousons look best, I think, with narrow bottoms—straight pants, leggings, or a straight skirt. If you're wearing pants, team them with a pair of short boots for a sophisticated finish.

Six Ways to Keep Warm

- Start with a cozy layer of large thermal cotton or silk-blend long johns. They feel good next to the skin and add an extra layer of warmth.

- Opt for many light layers rather than bulky clothes, which will make you feel more awkward and can overheat you, causing a chilling sweat.

- When it's really windy, choose a windbreaker as your outer layer.

- Keep head, feet, and hands covered. When they're warm, the whole body feels warmer. Use layers: leggings over socks, mittens over gloves, a wool scarf over a silk one.

- If a fur coat is out, add luxe—and warmth—with fur accessories. Hats, earmuffs, fur-lined gloves and boots are all available fairly reasonably.

- Take advantage of technology. Be sure to look for clothes made of cold-weather wonders like Gore-Tex and Thermolite to take the sting out of winter.

DENIM JACKETS

Another big style that can serve you well is the denim jacket. As with the blouson, nothing's sexier—now or later—than an oversized jacket above a narrow bottom. Add shoulder pads for balance and extra *oomph.* For warmth, wear lots of layers underneath. Aside from their status as true American classics, what I love about denim jackets is that they only get better with age. The more faded they are, the more comfortable they get—and the more attached to them you become. Wear them with jeans, of course. But also try them with straight skirts (the most flattering length depends on your shape, as shown at right), flowered Laura Ashley jumpers, white petticoats, men's shirts, or leggings.

Jacket liners, incidentally, can be a hardworking part of your wardrobe. These quilted linings—with or without sleeves— are available at army/navy shops. Use them to warm up any light jacket or vest or to insulate a sweatshirt jacket or an oversized blazer. Take the sleeves off an antique fur jacket and slide on a jacket liner with sleeves underneath for an informal effect. You can even sew two jacket liners together, adding a layer of polyester Fiberfil between the two, and wear the liner as outerwear.

As an alternative to denim for casual wraps, try duffle or stadium coats. Full-cut and unconstructed, made of heavy wool, with toggle buttons that close easily over pregnant bellies, these wraps add style to weekend wardrobes, keeping you warm, comfortable, and well protected. Move the closures over to add inches. For outdoor sporting events, you can't ask for a more fitting companion.

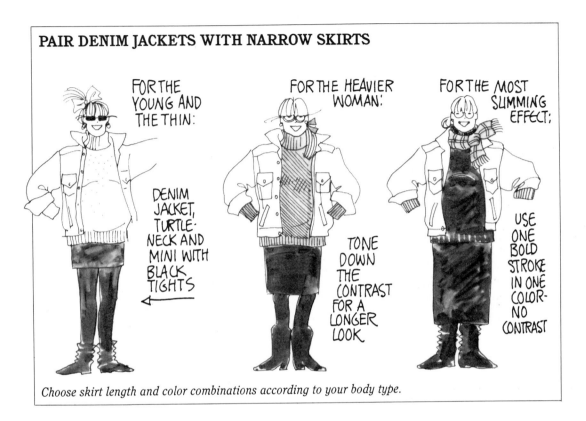

PAIR DENIM JACKETS WITH NARROW SKIRTS

FOR THE YOUNG AND THE THIN:

DENIM JACKET, TURTLENECK AND MINI WITH BLACK TIGHTS

FOR THE HEAVIER WOMAN:

TONE DOWN THE CONTRAST FOR A LONGER LOOK

FOR THE MOST SLIMMING EFFECT:

USE ONE BOLD STROKE IN ONE COLOR—NO CONTRAST

Choose skirt length and color combinations according to your body type.

THE ROMANCE OF SHAWLS

Shawls can be beautiful substitutes for lightweight jackets or coats, and they are certainly less expensive. In wool or challis, they're perfect for wearing to the office on a chilly spring or fall day, or for topping your modified or man's coat to add a feminine touch. In nubby wool or blanket plaids, they can be worn with jeans or pants or casual wool skirts. What could be prettier in the evening than a shawl edged in a cascade of ruffles or romanced with lace? Best of all, shawls are simple to make. A trip to your local fabric store can reveal dozens of possibilities. One 60-inch square of fabric hemmed and folded into a triangle will yield a shawl just right for throwing over your shoulders. If you like knitting or crocheting, shawls in many lovely patterns are easy, quick projects for evenings at home.

Staying Dry in Style

To ward off downpours and keep spirits high, here are two rainwear candidates for the bargain hall of fame. Both are made by Weather-Rite and were purchased at my local sporting goods shop for very reasonable prices. One is a rubberized nylon rain suit consisting of bib overalls and a hooded parka. The other is a soft plastic rain suit—hooded jacket and elastic-topped pants.

A Poncho-Style Coat to Make

Personally, I prefer ponchos to capes; I find them less constricting and easier to wear. One of my favorite maternity wraps was a modified poncho that I made from an inexpensive thermal blanket. In ivory, as pictured, the effect is quite casual. But imagine it made out of an elegant black blanket for evening. Or a red-and-black-plaid stadium blanket for a football game. The sewing's a cinch; you may notice that the directions are similar to those for the satin pouf dress described in Chapter 5. Here's how:

- Fold a twin-size blanket in half with wrong sides together, as shown, and casing at the bottom.

- Measure your head from ear to ear, adding two inches to get the neck opening measurement. Cut a slit to make the neck opening, as indicated. Sew a ready-made scarf, folded in half lengthwise, to the

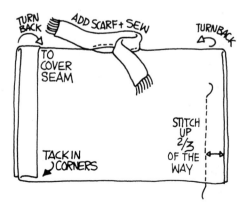

raw edge of the neck opening (right sides together), so it ties in front.

- Put the poncho on in order to gauge the correct width. Use straight pins to mark where your wrists are. Remove the poncho and stitch a vertical seam at the wrist line two-thirds of the way up both sides. (This leaves room for your arms.) Turn the edges back to cover the stitching and create a cuff, as illustrated, and tack the corners to finish.

- Try your new coat on. Let it flow or, if you prefer, put on a hip sash.

Both come in cheery yellow and fit pregnant bodies with ease. Personally, I can't think of better clothing ports in a storm. Tuck the pants into your socks and add bright plastic rainboots for a perfect finish.

If you need a longer raincoat for work, check your sporting goods or army/navy store for a long yellow slicker. Again, the price is right and the look is timeless.

Dime stores are also great places to look for rain gear. Check out the plastic raincoats and ponchos—often with matching hats. Just pick a cheery color and you can't go wrong.

Rubberized nylon overalls and a hooded parka in sunny yellow brighten a damp day.

Cold-Weather Skin Care

———

Keeping dry skin and chapped lips at bay is a reachable goal, but it requires consistent preventive care. This is especially important when you're pregnant, since skin problems do tend to flare up.

- Stock one pocket of every coat and bag with a tube of your preferred lip balm.

- Ease up on your cleansing technique. If you don't already, use tepid, rather than hot, water. Clean with fingertips only. Use a mild, lathering cleanser.

- Every so often, treat feet and hands to an intensive all-night softening session. Before bed, slather on lanolin cream or Vaseline, then cover with socks and gloves.

- Start moisturizing early in the season. Once the skin begins to flake, it takes three times longer to normalize it. Another way to protect against water loss is to switch from a water-base to an oil-base foundation for the winter. But check your skin type first.

- Stabilize moisture levels in the skin by using a humidifier at night.

- Keep a small container of your favorite moisturizer in your bag.

Knit a Knockout Sweater

Here's a chunky sweater that you can finish in practically no time. All you have to know is how to knit and purl in straight rows. There is no increasing or decreasing. Just knit each row, ending up with two large rectangles you then sew together. Sounds too easy to be beautiful, yet it works. And it's a sweater you'll enjoy wearing night after night—any time of the year. For evening, I like it done in metallic yarn mixed with cotton. The easy instructions are as follows:

- Cast 60 stitches of 16-ply yarn onto jumbo-sized needles. (This should give you 3 stitches per inch.) Knit and purl alternating rows until the rectangle reaches from your shoulders to your hips. Cast off. Make another rectangle exactly the same size.

- Sew the shoulder seams, leaving an opening large enough for your head. Divide the sides into thirds: Sew up the bottom two-thirds, leaving the top third open for your arms.

- If you want to control the fullness, thread a long ribbon through the bottom stitches and draw the sweater in at your hips. Add shoulder pads and layer your creation over a long-sleeved shirt or sweater, depending on how much warmth you need.

Going First Class with Fur

For quite a few of the pregnant women who responded to my questionnaire, a fur was the coat of choice. Many found that furs worked beautifully during pregnancy with no alterations needed—particularly if the coat was of recent vintage. As with other coats, new furs are being cut larger than ever.

If your coat doesn't fit, don't despair. Alyssa Rabach Anthone had an extra fur panel attached to the front of her raccoon coat and the hooks altered to fit. Madeline Kuflik didn't need any extra fur. Just moving the hooks an inch or two was enough. It's best to ask your furrier for suggestions.

Certainly, pregnancy is not the time to buy a brand-new fur. But if you've really got your heart set on a fur—and it can be a wonderful spirit-lifter—there are glorious ones available at secondhand shops across the country. You just need to know something about style and quality to find the best buys.

Fur-store manager and former maternity-store buyer Georgia Prstojevich recommends soft furs like fox or mink for versatility and wearability. To test for size, make sure the fur fits your upper back and shoulders, Georgia says, and you should have no trouble wearing the coat after your pregnancy. The Ritz Thrift Shop in New York City, famous for its sales on used furs, recommends fur capes for pregnant women in short-haired furs like beaver, nutria, and mink. Capes, the Ritz says, look good day and night and are an easy fit. Gloria Everhart, president of Act II Inc. in Kansas City, Missouri, agrees that short-haired furs are best: "A pregnant woman in a long-haired fur is going to look like a snowball." Magazine editor Judy Wederholt's friends were kinder. They just said she looked like a "fur Buddha" when she wore her secondhand beauty. Gloria Everhart advises checking out coats made from mink paws. They are both good-looking and well priced.

Properly cared for, furs can last 10 to 20 years or more. To see if the coat you're considering has stood the test of time:

• Make sure the fur has a nice sheen and feels supple.

• Look for consistent color. One coat is made of many skins that should be evenly matched.

• Check for worn spots. The most common wear areas are the collar, shoulders, and elbows. Some areas can be repaired, but it's often difficult to find fur matches for older coats.

• See how the coat feels on your body. It should feel fluid, not stiff.

• Notice the seams. There should be no visible breaks in the fur, and you should not be able to see into the underfur.

• The least important part of a fur coat is the lining. If everything else checks out and the lining is in tatters, buy the coat. Aside from hooks and eyes, a lining is the cheapest thing to replace.

While I was pregnant with my daughter, my husband bought me a gorgeous fox fling as a Christmas gift. A fling is a round tube of fur (often with tail and head on the ends) that you wrap around your neck like a scarf. It was really a perfect gift because it felt very luxurious yet was so practical. I could wear it over a sweater, on top of a cloth coat, with a suit—anything! And it made everything look great. If all that isn't enough, there's also the fact that flings don't get nearly the beating that fur coats do, so they last almost forever. And last but not least, they're much more affordable.

The keep-warm ideas you've read about in this chapter should help you settle on pregnancy outerwear that is both practical and chic. Be prepared with one rainwear outfit and at least two cold-weather wraps—one for work and formal occasions, and another for weekends. They'll keep you outdoors and active no matter what the weather.

CHAPTER 8

Accessories—the Secrets of Style

Scarves, jewelry, hats, gloves, purses, socks, and shoes all play starring roles in a maternity wardrobe. One of their functions is to help add interest and variation to the more limited choices of clothing you have now. Another is that of illusion. If the accessory is bold, big, or interesting enough, it can help draw the eye away from the tummy area and toward the face, neck, wrists, or feet. Any accessory you buy while pregnant will give you just as much pleasure after the baby is born. Accessories are also wonderful ways to create new outfits without making major purchases. So you can splurge a bit, knowing that your money is well spent.

Nowhere is your personal style more evident than in your choice of accessories. Some women love wearing lots of necklaces and hate anything on their wrists. Some wear silk scarves and no jewelry whatsoever. Others focus on a great-looking bag or an eye-catching pair of shoes. Pregnancy doesn't affect these preferences very much except as far as proportion is concerned. You need to focus on scale; make your accessories relate to your body as well as to your outfit. The delicate little silk square you used to wear with all your suits may look lost above a billowy expanse of tummy. Your thin gold chain can look inconsequential. An absolutely wonderful shoulder bag may hit you at exactly the wrong spot. And you may find that your wide-brimmed hat adds width you don't need right now.

Rather than giving up accessories that no longer seem right, try them on in different ways. It may be, for example, that your thin gold chain looks fine if worn in concert with six others of graduated length. Or teamed with a strand of pearls. Your small silk scarf may be banished from your neck, but it can do maternity duty as a pocket square. And you may be able to attach a new, longer strap to your shoulder bag so it hits you at a more flattering spot.

Generally speaking, the accessories you wear now should be bolder, brighter, and positioned well away from the tummy (which gets all the attention it needs as a matter of course).

Jewelry

Whether you love real jewelry or costume, the key is to present a consistent image. Jewelry should relate in texture, color, mood, size, and shape to other pieces you're wearing and to your clothes as well. Brightly painted ceramic earrings worn with pearls won't work. The first are artsy and fun, the latter classic and dressed up. But teaming the same ceramic earrings with hand-painted beads and a colorful cotton shirt can look smashing. The same jewelry worn against a serious silk blouse would look all wrong.

NECKLACES— THE RIGHT LENGTH

For most women, short or choker-style necklaces look best during pregnancy because they create a tighter focus on the face. If you are petite or have a short neck, wear your necklaces a little longer, but still above the bosom, to create a longer, slimmer look. All pregnant women should avoid necklaces that extend into the bumpy zone created by bust and tummy. Best to let fabric alone smooth over those areas.

You can still don your longer necklaces without doubling them up—if you wear them with backless dresses. Hang several strands of beads down the back to accentuate a part of your body that *hasn't* changed.

As you've done with clothing, add whimsy to accessories. Your new condition is an excuse for indulging a sense of playfulness in casual settings. Wear bunches of touristy necklaces, replete with images of the Statue of Liberty, the Eiffel Tower, or the Golden Gate Bridge. Airport shops are great places for this kind of bounty. Ask traveling friends to bring some home for you. Pick up long strands of pearls from street vendors or discount shops and wind them around your neck. The more the better.

As an interesting alternative to necklaces, try bolo ties. These western necklaces are favorite accessories of mine, and they give a nice lengthening line in front. You don't have to buy the real McCoy to enjoy their look. Try improvising one with a string of beads or a shoelace—gathered up in a brooch that you pin to your collar. As a variation, draw two ends of a cotton scarf through a ring, making sure it's secure and letting the ends hang free in front.

EARRINGS

To further tighten the focus on your face while you're pregnant, make heavy use of earrings. One former model found that "larger earrings complemented my rounder face" during pregnancy. Housewife Mary Ernst says she found herself "more interested in earrings and less interested in other jewelry." Earrings with the right color can make your skin look rosier. They also adorn without getting in the way (except possibly when you're on the phone). Unlike necklaces and bracelets, earrings don't really surround or enclose an area and are therefore less confining.

Making the right choice in earrings is important. Since they are worn very close to your eyes, earrings can really enhance eye color and shine if you're careful to select a complementary shade. Here are some of the best earring-eye combinations:

• Sapphire and aquamarine with blue eyes

- Emerald and hazel tones with green eyes

- Topaz or gray with brown eyes

- Black onyx or crystal with black eyes

If you have cool, blue undertones in your skin, silver, platinum, or white gold look best. If your skin is warm and golden, wear yellow gold, bronze, or copper.

Earring shape is important, too. Button styles are best on women with long necks because they keep eyes focused on the face. Conversely, dangling earrings can have a lengthening effect on short necks. Consider your hairstyle as well. Sizable button earrings are best with short hair; small or dangling types for longer hairstyles. If you wear glasses, realize that they are accessories, too. Adding large earrings and necklaces can create clutter if you're not careful.

Make Your Own Earrings

Perk up your maternity wardrobe with some quick fixes that are frivolous and fun. String little colored beads onto your hoop earrings, changing colors according to what you're wearing. Attach a post to a pretty antique button for instant—and genuine— button earrings. Canvas flea markets and second-hand shops for baubles and beads that you can adapt easily to your ears.

Scarves and Wraps

As you've no doubt noticed by now, I made heavy use of scarves during my pregnancies. I have a whole collection, which I add to every time I catch sight of a new color. One of the most useful types is the oblong length of cotton gauze you can pick up in Indian clothing shops. I use them as hip wraps, neckties, and head wraps. You can even tie them onto the handles of an old bag to use as a strap. Since the scarves are made of cotton, they're comfortable and not at all scratchy. I love the look of several colors twisted together and worn around the neck.

If you long for some luxury, consider indulging yourself in a "status" scarf. You may not be able to wear clothing by Hermès, Chanel, Gucci, or Yves Saint Laurent when you're pregnant, but you can certainly wear their scarves. (To create blouses out of them for the office, see page 66.) One magazine editor I know who treated herself to a Hermès scarf said it actually drew more comments than her tummy. Because she wore it so often while she was pregnant and continues to do so now, the cost per wear has turned out to be quite little.

If you want to send a feminine message, nothing does it faster than lace. Lace scarves are an especially good choice for pregnancy because they're practically weightless. They provide a lot of effect with very little bulk. Antique scarves look particularly pretty. (You can achieve an antique look with new lace by soaking it for half an hour in lukewarm tea and hanging it up to dry.) Combine lace with pearls. Lace with denim. Even lace with a cotton T-shirt. Soften the look of a man's

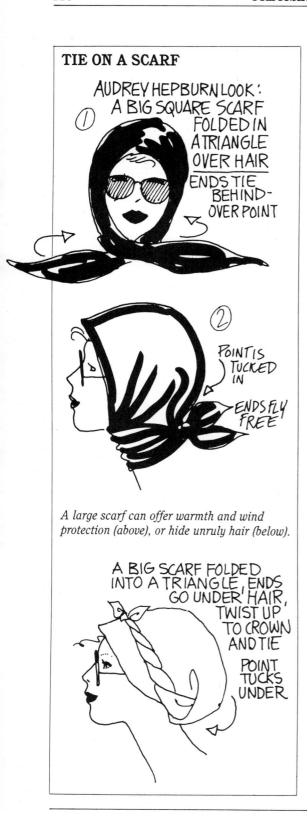

TIE ON A SCARF

AUDREY HEPBURN LOOK:
① A BIG SQUARE SCARF FOLDED IN A TRIANGLE OVER HAIR

ENDS TIE BEHIND- OVER POINT

② POINT IS TUCKED IN

ENDS FLY FREE

A large scarf can offer warmth and wind protection (above), or hide unruly hair (below).

A BIG SCARF FOLDED INTO A TRIANGLE, ENDS GO UNDER HAIR, TWIST UP TO CROWN AND TIE

POINT TUCKS UNDER

shirt and jacket with a length of lace tied in a bow under the shirt collar. Romance a simple pullover by wrapping an oblong piece of lace around the neck several times and fastening it with a cameo or other antique-looking pin.

As I mentioned in Chapter 4, the impact of almost any dress can be increased tenfold by draping an oversized silk scarf or shawl over one shoulder. Instant sophistication. If you like, you can fasten it at the shoulder with a brooch. For another variation, pull the scarf diagonally across the dress and tie it at the hips. On a more casual outfit, tie the arms of a pullover or sweatshirt—in a contrasting or matching color—across your body in the same way for an extra shot of color, texture—interest!

Feminize borrowed menswear with scarves of all types. Add luxury to cotton men's shirts with soft silk charmeuse bows. Or tuck a long thin scarf under the collar of a man's jacket to offset and soften the tailored lines. Once you learn to use scarves, you'll wonder how you ever dressed without them.

Finally, don't overlook the practical uses of scarves. A cheery fuchsia one, for example, can brighten up your olive drab trench coat—and keep your neck warm at the same time. Wrap a large scarf around your head and neck, as shown at upper left, to keep spring or fall breezes at bay. Or, anytime you'd rather not fool with your hair, use a big colorful scarf as a head wrap. Fold it into a triangle. Holding the two folded ends, place the long edge at your forehead and bring the ends to the back of your neck, under your hair. Cross them and bring them back up to your crown, twisting as illustrated at left. Tuck in the point—and your hair—in back and let the winds blow!

Pretty, Practical Hats

When you're pregnant, think of hats as an opportunity to add a note of sleekness to a silhouette that is anything but slim. The hat mistake that many pregnant women make is going for a broad brim, which only adds another wide line. Choose from among the following styles and you can't go wrong.

FOR LONG OR SHORT HAIR— A FELT OR STRAW HAT IN A LARGE SIZE

LONG OR SHORT HAIR— TUCK INTO YOUR BIG BERET

• Berets fill the bill perfectly. They're classic, easy to wear, and relatively affordable. Tuck most of your hair in, letting just a few wisps escape. Or experiment with various angles, shaping the fabric to flatter your face. Wear berets as they are or decorate them to suit your style. The easiest add-on is any kind of pin or brooch. Search your mother's or grandmother's jewelry box for inexpensive old pins. Or completely cover your beret with tourist pins and political buttons. Sew on military emblems. For evening, glue some rhinestones onto a white, royal blue, red, or black beret.

• Soft felt brimmed hats can be customized, too. Buy them secondhand at thrift shops. Pin badges around the crown. Glue on feathers. Pin back a brim with a brooch to alter the shape. Tie a scarf or ribbon around the brim. Wear it at a provocative angle.

FOR LONG HAIR

TUCK YOUR HAIR UP

• I have a passion for caps. As I mentioned in Chapter 6, my favorites tend to come from sporting goods shops, not department stores. Whenever I travel, it's the sporting goods shops I hit first. I have fishing hats from Italy, cricket caps from Australia, and baseball caps from the States. Most are useful as well as good-looking, and searching them out is a fun way to get beyond the typical tourist offerings. Nothing looks more feminine on a woman's face than a macho man's hat. If you have long hair, tuck it under the cap.

CUFFED
KNIT HAT
FOR
ANY
LENGTH
HAIR

they make even the cheapest cloth coat luxurious. If you tend to avoid hats because of the way they scrunch your hair, consider fur earmuffs as a fancy—and practical—alternative.

PERUVIAN SKI HAT (KNIT)

WORKS
FOR
LONG OR
SHORT
HAIR

• For variety in casual caps, try some of the more unusually shaped knit ones you'll find in ski or specialty shops, like the Peruvian ski hat illustrated here.

LET YOUR
HAIR TAKE
THE PLACE
OF THE
CROWN IN
A STRAW
HAT

• Because they fit close, knit caps are flattering to pregnant silhouettes. Try one with a thick cuff for warmth and a nice frame around your face. Another idea for a sub-zero day is to pair up a ski hat and a knit scarf. Pull the scarf on first, muffling it around your neck. Then, pull the ski hat on top for handsome double coverage over your ears.

• It's hard to beat the look—and feeling—of fur around your face. Fur-lined Russian-style hats are great-looking and terrifically warm. Combined with a fur scarf or collar,

• Try straw hats for summer. Remember to keep them narrow-brimmed, except when they're serving as sunshades. An idea for natural blondes: Trim away the crown of a worn-out hat, leaving just the brim, and pull your hair through. This way you can let the sun lighten your hair without burning your face.

Best Bags

Most women are accustomed to wearing shoulder bags, which, unfortunately, tend to hit pregnant bodies at precisely the widest, most unflattering spot. The solution is to look for a very long bag that hits somewhere near the top of your thigh. If you're in love with your present bag, adapt it by having a new strap made. Straps of chain can usually be added quite easily.

What I preferred while I was pregnant were clutch bags. Tucked under your arm, they add no bulk. I often used a leather envelope of my husband's—designed for holding a sheaf of papers and not much more. The stuff I piled in stretched its original purpose, but it still did the job beautifully.

If I had to carry a lot of things, I switched over to a leather carryall, shaped like a shopping bag. It was big enough to allow me to consolidate. It held an extra pair of shoes, my clutch bag, newspaper, work, plus a morning muffin. The effect was much sleeker than carrying a separate bag for each item.

Another bag I couldn't function without was a nylon duffle—the kind you find at any sports shop. They come in all sorts of great colors and cost very little. And they expand to tote cargo of practically any size.

For casual use, I've always loved the look of a hobo bag. You can make one to fit anything you have to carry, and the price is right. The bag is yours for the price of a square of fabric. Of course, you may already own a suitable scarf, in which case the bag comes to you absolutely free, a notion true to its hobo beginnings. It makes a perfect picnic bag, too, acting as both hamper and tablecloth. I suggested the idea to one friend who immediately made them in a slew of colors, then went on to use them after the baby was born.

A 36-inch square creates a nice size bag. Lay the square out flat on a table, as shown. Pile your belongings on top. Then pick up two opposite corners and tie them tightly in the center. Tie the two remaining corners loosely to create a handle. Sling it over your shoulder and you're on your way.

THE HOBO BAG

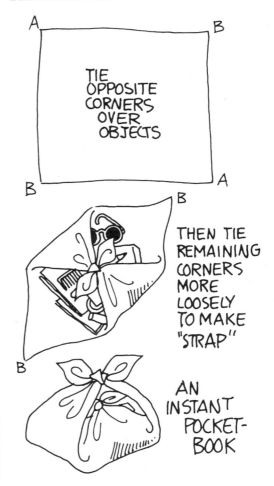

A — B

TIE OPPOSITE CORNERS OVER OBJECTS

B — A

B

THEN TIE REMAINING CORNERS MORE LOOSELY TO MAKE "STRAP"

B

AN INSTANT POCKETBOOK

Turn a big scarf into an all-purpose carryall in seconds.

Make a Tube Hat

You can buy a wool tube hat—the kind that starts like a cowl around your neck, then pulls up into a hat—to keep your ears and neck well protected. Or you can make a soft cotton one—as I did—out of an old pair of warm-up pants. Simply cut one leg off at the thigh and again about 15 inches down, creating a tube. You needn't even hem the raw edges; they'll roll back neatly all by themselves after one washing. Wear the tube as a cowl until the wind really howls. Then pull it up onto your head for maximum protection.

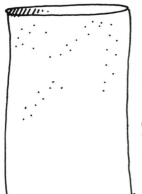

A LEG FROM A PAIR OF SWEAT-PANTS MAKES A GREAT TUBE HAT

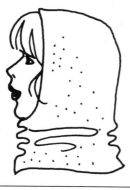

Fingerless gloves over contrasting whole gloves create a cheery effect while keeping you extra warm. Mix and match for variety.

Gloves

Living on and off in Paris over the years has given me the opportunity to observe French women rather closely. And although I'm no closer to figuring out what gives them that certain *je ne sais quoi*, I have taken a few notes. For one thing, French women wear gloves winter, spring, summer, and fall. I don't know why, but gloves are sexy. And because they draw attention away from the belly, they're a wonderful accessory for pregnant women.

To achieve the proper effect, you must go beyond mundane wool gloves to crocheted lace, cotton, spandex, and colored leathers. Gloves don't have to be pricey. In fact, they shouldn't be. Everyone knows a matched pair of gloves is never long for this earth. So buy cheap and enjoy them while the pair lasts. Check antique clothing shops, five-and-dime stores, sales bins. Or go to the other extreme and invest in a pair of designer gloves that will up your spirits.

Here are just a few suggestions for injecting style with gloves:

• To add chic to a denim jacket, wear driving gloves, an oversized watch, a chiffon scarf, and sunglasses—all in black.

• Focus on the wrist. Wear wrist-length white cotton gloves. Buckle a watch over one glove and stack three gold chains over the other.

• Tuck a pair of lace gloves—or just the one you have left—in a breast pocket. Use it in the brim of a hat. Or in a belt.

• Pull on long leather gloves in a rich, dark color to give special elegance to your everyday wool coat.

Umbrellas

You may not think of umbrellas as accessories, but they can be as pretty as they are useful. Umbrellas with straps are best, but they tend to be more expensive than the ones without. What I do is attach a pretty ribbon or braid to both ends—knots are all you need to secure it—and sling it over my shoulder. A ribbon is nicer than most of the straps around, anyway. This method has kept me from losing umbrellas—which I used to do endlessly—and it also keeps my hands free.

Good old canvas umbrellas do the job, but you can also find pretty oriental ones made of waterproofed paper. These usually are embellished with flowers, and they make wonderful parasols for keeping the sun off in the summer.

The Shoes to Choose

Some women's feet don't change at all during pregnancy. Others' increase a full size or more. But whether their feet grew or stayed the same, nearly all the women I spoke with found themselves wearing sneakers—good, supportive ones—far more than they ever thought they would. They wore them at home; they wore them to work. They wore them out—in both senses of the word.

How much your feet will change depends on a variety of factors, including how much weight you gain, how strong your arches are, and the amount of water you retain. Some experts theorize that a woman's foot changes during pregnancy to give her increased stability. Dr. Peter J. Torotora, a Connecticut podiatrist, believes that most of the foot problems connected with pregnancy can be traced to rapid weight gain. "What other time in your life do you gain thirty pounds in the space of less than nine months?"

Dr. Torotora warns that if you do have any foot problems, pregnancy will exaggerate them. But he rejects the idea of having special orthotics made, except in very special situations. "In most cases, any problem will disappear as soon as the baby is born and your weight returns to normal, so the expense isn't warranted," he advises.

"Instead, get yourself a comfortable, supportive shoe." One of the best solutions is the crop of walking sneakers being produced by the major companies. Usually made of leather for breathability, they offer terrific support and comfort.

Much as we might like to, most of us can't wear sneakers nonstop. What are the alternatives? Corporate lawyer Madeline Kuflik stopped wearing even low heels sometime in the sixth month. She switched to flats by a company called Rockport, which she says are "incredibly comfortable." Publicist Alyssa Rabach Anthone, who was pregnant during the winter, wore boots a lot. She felt that "there were fewer seams and places to cut the foot." A French painter lived in well-worn cowboy boots. One saleswoman who has to be on her feet a lot didn't think she could get away with traditional sneakers, so she was thrilled to find her favorites in black leather. When she wore them with pants you really didn't notice they weren't regular shoes.

If you're hesitant to invest in shoes because you're not sure what size your foot will be after pregnancy, try buying just one pair of very plain, relatively inexpensive, ultra-comfortable pumps in a neutral cranberry color that you can wear with everything. (You can add variety to these sensible shoes in the stockings you choose and with shoe clips. See ideas about the latter on page 73.)

Consider carefully any pair of shoes you buy now. Choose the most versatile style you can find in a color that goes with everything in your wardrobe. And make it a shoe that looks as good at night as it does during the day. A tall order, granted. But a little extra shopping can save you a lot of extra money.

Flying Tip

Flying tends to cause feet to swell, compounding your pregnancy problems. It's best to wear lace-up shoes and take them off as soon as you're seated. Then, if your feet do swell, you'll be able to loosen the laces and walk off the plane in comfort. I learned this lesson from experience: I once wore a pair of pumps onto the plane and three hours later couldn't get my feet back into them. I was forced to walk off the plane barefoot!

LOOKING FOR COMFORT

According to Dr. Torotora, suede and kid leather shoes are exceptionally comfortable because they have a lot of give and they mold to your feet with wear. Resist buying shoes made of patent leather and synthetic materials because they won't stretch at all. This would not normally be a problem if the shoe fit perfectly. But when you're pregnant and your foot is apt to swell and change, a shoe with no give may cause blisters and callouses.

Another thing you should look for in a shoe is support. Dr. Torotora likes the idea of wearing a good running shoe around the house, on weekends, and on the way to and from work. "If your feet get good support like that the majority of the time, you can wear what you like for short stretches in between." Before I became pregnant, I used to live in old-fashioned canvas tennis shoes. As I got bigger, my feet began to ache and I realized I just wasn't getting the support I needed around my arches. That's when I discovered Reeboks. And I wore them just about everywhere after that. Now, of course, lots of manufacturers are making good-looking leather sneakers in great colors.

What about heels? Your legs and back will be the best judges, but you can wear moderately high heels when you won't be standing for long periods of time. I wore them mostly to dinner parties and business meetings. If I was invited to a cocktail party, I went in flats. "Heels over two or three inches are too unstable for most people," says Dr. Torotora. "And the increased weight brings too much pressure to bear on the metatarsals. It is a good idea, however, to vary heel heights between the flat to two-inch range—some variety in heel height is good for your legs."

When you shop for shoes, don't worry about driving the salesperson crazy—take your time choosing the right ones. To avoid the "Gee, they felt great this morning" blues, shop in the afternoon, when your feet are most swollen and hardest to fit. Any shoe that feels great then is bound to be a winner. See if you can wiggle your toes easily. That's a good sign because the most important fit point is at the front of the foot. Another front-of-the-foot check is to stomp on the floor. You shouldn't be able to feel your toes against the front of the toe box. Now take the shoe off and hold the sole up to the sole of your foot. If your foot is wider than the shoe, you're asking for trouble. Check the insides of the shoe for smooth finishing. Ragged linings and bulky seams are potential irritators. Next, set the shoe up on its heel. Using your index finger, press down on the toe. The more easily the shoe bends, the more comfortable it will feel.

If your foot seems to fall somewhere between sizes—the smaller feels a bit tight, the larger a bit big—go for the larger size. A tight shoe will only feel tighter the longer you've got it on.

SHOES ON A SHOESTRING

There are some casual, comfortable shoes you can buy while you're pregnant without jeopardizing your bank account. They're found in the discount stores I praised in Chapter 3. Stay away from synthetic copies of more formal styles, but plunge ahead into the bins of cotton sneakers and rubber beach thongs. They're perfect for wearing around the house, yard, or playground on warm afternoons. If you need more support as the months go on, switch back to leather walking shoes.

Plain white sneakers are so inexpensive at discount stores that you can indulge in them guilt free. Here are some ways to dress them up.

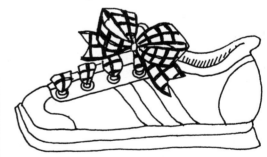

GINGHAM OR PLAID RIBBON FOR LACES

• Replace the laces with satin, lace, grosgrain, polka-dot, or plaid ribbon.

• Cut out the toes for extra coolness and a fun look.

• Dye the shoes pastel colors by throwing them in a basin of dye.

• Glue on rhinestones or glitter.

Sole Soothers

With the extra load that pregnancy puts on your feet, swelling, tiredness, aches, and pains all become common complaints. These treatments will help soothe your soles.

- Elevate your feet to relieve tiredness and swelling. If you sit at a desk, place a stool underneath and put your feet up whenever possible.

- At night, treat your feet to a soak. The best recipe for relieving tiredness, swelling, and that achy feeling—according to Dr. Torotora—is plain old table salt (or Epsom salts) in warm water. Use one teaspoon per pint.

- Get yourself one of those wooden rollers designed for foot massages, available at health-food stores. Run your feet over the roller whenever they feel tired or uncomfortable. It feels wonderful and is even discreet enough to do under your desk.

- You or your husband can knead your feet. Let what feels good be your guide. You might include gentle circles using thumb and fingers along the top and sole of the foot. Apply hard pressure with thumbs across the ball of the foot and down the center from the ball to the heel. And finally, rub and pull each toe individually.

- Moisturize your feet often—twice a day, if possible. When you're pregnant, your feet tend to become drier and are more prone to cracking due to swelling. Also, moisturized feet are less apt to rub against shoes and blister.

- Before putting shoes on, apply powder to the sole of the shoe to absorb perspiration and help resist athlete's foot. This is a better method than applying powder directly to the foot, where it tends to ball and collect—uncomfortably—between the toes.

- Relax your feet with this technique: Sit with your right ankle crossed over your left knee. Slip the fingers of your left hand through your toes. Gently squeeze and release several times. Repeat on the opposite side.

- Refresh your feet with astringent or witch hazel. I was pregnant in the summer, and my feet were uncomfortably hot all the time. I always carried a bottle of astringent and a few cotton balls so I could dab some around my ankles and on the soles of my feet whenever the heat got to me. It felt wonderfully cool and stimulating.

• Sponge paint them with tempera paint and a kitchen sponge.

• Use felt-tip markers to draw on polka dots or stripes.

The rubber thongs you can buy at dime stores are cheap and comfortable, but not terribly attractive. Here's a redo that'll make a pair more fun to wear: Pick up a few yards of ribbon in your favorite solid color, or in polka dots, plaid, or stripes.

Then wind the ribbon around the rubber, as shown. For a whimsical touch, add ballerina ties by knotting two 36-inch pieces of ribbon on the straps and criss-crossing them around your ankles.

Learn to Love Socks

Some women are notorious shoe addicts. For them, the prospect of quashing the shoe-buying impulse for nine months is almost unbearable. One friend and fellow shoe addict had a novel idea: transfer my affections from shoes to socks for the duration. And it worked.

One thing that helped me along is the fact that socks have become truly a lot more fun in the past few years. Without even looking hard, you can find polka-dotted, striped, flowered, plaid, painted, beaded, textured, and appliquéd socks. You can collect socks by your favorite designer. If you have the good fortune to be traveling or know someone who is going to Italy, ask her to check out the sock departments for you. Italian socks are gems—the best quality and design in the world! It's a brave new sock world out there, inviting inventive combinations. Try striped socks with flowered shoes. Polka-dotted socks with bright red flats. Socks under sandals—more comfortable than bare for sweaty, pregnant feet. Above all, socks are an addiction even a penny-pincher can enjoy.

Employed as camouflage, socks can work wonders. Keep swollen ankles under wraps by bunching soft cotton socks down around the ankles. Are your socks too bulky for your shoes? Wear thin cotton socks and cut a pair of bulky ones off at the ankles to form a tube. Pull the tube on and bunch it around your ankle.

Pamper Your Feet with a Pedicure

If those I talked to are any indication, pregnant women alone could keep the nation's pedicurists in business. Pedicures were hands down the most frequently mentioned beauty treat—for a couple of good reasons. One is that feet become progressively more difficult to reach comfortably. And, as the months go by, your feet just hurt more, so a pedicure and the accompanying foot soak and massage feel especially welcome. Here's one recommendation: While one foot is being worked on, request a stool for the other one, just to keep circulation on an even keel.

Since you won't always get to the pedicurist as often as you might like, here's how to do it yourself in between times—as long as you can reach your feet!

- Start by soaking feet in warm, mild, sudsy water for up to five minutes.

- Pat your feet dry and cover the cuticles with cuticle cream.

- Push the cuticles back gently with an orange stick.

- Cut or file the nails straight across.

- Massage moisturizer into the entire foot, pressing hard on the ball of the foot and any sore spots.

- Take a length of cotton twice the width of your foot and wind it between your toes.

- Apply one coat of clear and then two coats of your favorite polish. Clear, bright shades of red and pink help to minimize puffiness and make feet look pretty and well cared for. Nice!

Preventing Varicose Veins

Somewhere between 10 and 20 percent of all pregnant women get varicose veins. The reason, according to Ronald Dee, M.D., assistant clinical professor of surgery at Albert Einstein College of Medicine in New York City, is that the hormones released during early pregnancy can relax the veins, and make their valves less efficient. Quite often, the veins recover when the pregnancy is over. However, a family history of varicose veins puts you at greater risk, and you should take precautions. Dr. Dee recommends consistent daily use of support stockings. (You shouldn't wear them at night.) Don't bother with department-store-style support hose—they're not strong enough to give the leg the compression needed.

Support hose are available in both panty hose and knee-high styles. For purposes of protection, knee-highs are sufficient. How do support stockings work? The stockings squeeze the veins from outside, which helps prevent them from stretching and becoming varicose.

The best exercise for preventing varicose veins is walking, which keeps the blood pumping and prevents it from collecting in the legs. Sitting with your feet up for an hour can relieve discomfort, but it does nothing for the veins. As Dr. Dee explains, "After all, when you sleep your legs are up for a good eight hours. What could one hour more possibly accomplish?"

From hats to shoes, accessories can make the difference between just being dressed and looking wonderfully pulled to-

Wear moderately high heels if you feel comfortable, but not if you'll be standing for long periods of time.

gether. They are crucial elements in your maternity wardrobe, and choosing and using them can be fun as well as economical. Do some fashion brainstorming to expand on the ideas I've given here, and get ready to accept some compliments!

CHAPTER 9

Lingerie That Really Works

As polished as you may appear on the surface, if the straps of your bra are digging into your shoulders or your panty hose are slipping down your thighs, you certainly won't feel as good as you look. As every pregnant woman soon discovers, lingerie that fits well and feels comfortable is not a luxury—it's a necessity. This chapter is a guide to gathering the lingerie you need, with tips on shopping, fitting, and keeping it all in shape.

Starting at the Top—Bras

As your body prepares to nurse your developing baby, hormones will cause your breast size to increase by a cup size or more. This means you're going to be needing some new bras. As your breasts enlarge, they will get heavier as well, and this added weight will put a strain on the fragile ligaments supporting your breasts.

The more support and protection you can give your breasts from the beginning of your pregnancy, the better chance you'll have of forestalling droop and keeping your shape in the future.

Depending on how you grow, you may go through several different sizes during the course of your pregnancy. Don't worry; you'll make double use of the extra bras you may have to buy because you can wear them postpregnancy, too, while your breasts are returning to normal size. Whether you choose regular or maternity styles, purchasing a supportive bra in the right size is one of the best body moves you can make.

SIZING YOURSELF UP

According to lingerie industry sources, 70 to 90 percent of all women wearing bras are wearing the wrong size. To escape from this unenlightened majority, and also because your size is likely to change, it's a good idea to be able to measure yourself. You can go to a good lingerie department and have a professional do it for you, but following these simple instructions can save you the trip.

First, measure around your chest—with your regular bra on—by holding the tape measure under your arms but above your bust. The tape should be pulled snug but not squeezed. This measurement is the bra size—30, 34, 36, etc. If the measurement is an odd number, round it up to the next bra size. A woman whose chest measures 33, for instance, would take a 34 bra.

To determine your cup size, measure your bust at its fullest point. If this measurement is less than 1½ inches larger than your bra size, an A cup is indicated. If the measurement is 1½ to 2½ inches larger, you're a B cup; 2½ to 3½ inches larger, a C; 3½ to 4½ inches larger, a D;

Two Notions Worth Knowing About

If you want to wear your regular bras as long as possible, consider using bra extenders. These are pieces of fabric with an extra couple of hooks sewn on that you can attach to the back of your bra to add an inch or so. They can be found in notions departments. Use them wisely, however. If the cups in your old bra are just too small, it's worth buying a new one to get the support you need.

If your bra is creating painful ridges on your shoulders, try placing shoulder pads under the straps to eliminate discomfort. The pads will shape your shirts at the same time!

4½ to 5½ inches larger, an E (maternity) or DD (regular); and 5½ to 6½ inches larger, an F (maternity) or EE (regular). For example, if your chest measures 34 and your bust 37, you should wear a 34C, since the difference is 3 inches.

Plan to measure yourself at three-month intervals throughout your pregnancy, and during the nursing period, to monitor your size. Maternity, or prenatal, and nursing bras (more on these later) have a certain amount of adaptability built in, but there comes a point when a new size is definitely indicated.

Christina Johnson of Olga, a leading lingerie company, is Olga's daughter and the mother of two children herself. She says, "When you start feeling restricted and unsupported, it's time for a change. Don't wait until you're spilling out of the cups, the underwire is poking into your flesh, the straps are leaving red marks, and the bra feels tight and uncomfortable everywhere."

If you have any questions about fit or size, find out where the best bra-fitters are in your area and go see them. Good department stores usually have educated lingerie saleswomen. Speciality shops are another good bet. One woman I spoke with had her first professional bra fitting during her pregnancy. After trying on all kinds of bras, she was guided to a style that really fit well and felt good. She finished her pregnancy in well-supported comfort and feels "the extra expense was well worth it."

RECOGNIZING GOOD SUPPORT

If you decide to stick with regular bras throughout your pregnancy, do make sure that the ones you choose give you the

Maternity and Nursing Bras

Here are some of the most comfortable styles. Top (left to right): Leading Lady's seamed maternity bra; Japanese Weekend's "O.K." style;

Leading Lady's smooth maternity bra. Bottom: Nursing bras by Olga (left) and Leading Lady.

WIDE BACKS →

ATHLETIC STYLING WITH NURSING ACCESS

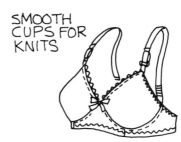

SMOOTH CUPS FOR KNITS

FOLDS TO SIDE AND TUCKS OUT OF THE WAY

BECAUSE THIS BRA SNAPS— YOU CAN OPEN IT ONE-HANDED!

UNHOOK AND OPEN

support you need. Here are some tests: Touch the top of your breasts while you're wearing the bra. Does the skin feel supported, or stretched? Cup your breasts in your hands through the bra. If you can lift them at all, chances are the bra is allowing your breasts to sag too much. Look for a bra that lifts you. Last, do the jiggle test. Jump up and down—carefully. Do your breasts move a lot or do they stay pretty steady? If you're getting adequate support and coverage, there should be very little movement.

Look for support features like wide straps (over ⅜-inch) and wide backs and sides. Underwires are a top choice for support-seekers both large and small. If you've avoided underwires because of an impression that they're stiff and uncomfortable, try one on. You'll probably be surprised. The new ones are so thin and flexible you can tie them in knots. If you're large, underwires ease the weight off your shoulders. If you're small, they offer lift and contour.

Fabric is a key support factor, too. Tightly woven fabrics or tight knits are best. Before you buy, check the grain of the fabric. If it runs diagonally across the cup, you can expect super support—much more than if the fabric runs straight across or up and down. Sometimes seams across the cup are a good indication of support. They can reinforce the cup and accommodate more breast tissue.

Christina likes the feeling of cotton when she's pregnant. "It's more comfortable against your skin." According to Christina, cotton is a "forgiving fiber." A cotton bra will grow with you, giving you a little bit longer wear. She feels that "molded cotton cups with a little Lycra in them are the best."

MATERNITY BRAS— HELP OR HYPE?

When I was pregnant, I wore my regular bras as long as I could and then switched to a larger size. I had never heard of maternity bras, nor had most of the women with whom I spoke. I'm sorry now that I hadn't.

The fact is, the more I found out about maternity, or prenatal, bras (the terms are interchangeable) in the course of my research for this book, the more I liked the idea. No longer are they the ugly, "harness"-type contraptions they used to be. Prenatal bras can save you money because they come with four fasteners in back instead of three. This gives you the grace of one extra fastener before it's necessary to buy a new set of bras. For another, they really do take care of your breasts. Maternity bras have wider sides for more support, so there's no sag under the bra cup or under the arm, and no stretching on top of the bust. That's very important. The backs of prenatal bras are stretchier and more elastic to allow for expansion. And the shoulder straps are soft and elasticized, to carry the weight without digging in.

According to Cathy Foley of Leading Lady, one of the nation's biggest makers of maternity bras: "The sooner the breasts are properly supported, the more you can inhibit the stretch marks and breast droop that so often occur in pregnancy." A prenatal bra can be used just as soon as you notice a swelling or tenderness in your breasts. (For many women, those two symptoms are the first signs of pregnancy.) Cathy recommends buying the size that feels comfortable on the tightest hooks. Then you've got three more sets of hooks to go before you need the next size.

Prenatal bras are usually carried in maternity departments rather than lingerie sections—one reason many women miss out on them. Maternity shops often carry them as well.

NURSING BRAS

Nursing bras, like the rest of maternity wear, have undergone a lot of reevaluation in the past few years. When new mothers

---

Breastfeeding in Public—A Modest Proposal

Although some women have no qualms about breastfeeding in public, others feel uncomfortably exposed. Being one of the latter, I was glad to discover a way to nurse in relative privacy on a 747—or in any other crowded situation: Wear a T-shirt or tank under a button-up shirt. Pull the T up and the unbuttoned shirt over so that only the feeding area is exposed.

talk, manufacturers apparently do listen. In many cases, the result is bras that are appealing to look at, available in a range of fabrics from comfortable cotton to sexy lace, and, above all, easier to use.

The newest bra is one Christina of Olga came up with during her second pregnancy. The design is based on requirements she had defined while nursing her first baby. For women who expect a nursing bra to look and feel like a harness, Christina's is a revelation. Made of a soft stretch cotton blend—to adapt to daily size fluctuations—it looks more like a sport bra than anything else. A unique feature is the cup construction: the cups snap open from the center rather than the top, and fold to the side and out of the way for nursing. (See illustration on page 133.) Sizes range from 34B to 38D.

Leading Lady's enormous range of sizes and styles runs the gamut from all cotton to lacy nylon types. They all sport the patented Fastnurs fastener, which some women find a cinch to maneuver, others a chore. Marketing director Cathy Foley says it's just a matter of being shown the correct technique from the onset. She strongly recommends asking the saleswoman for a demonstration. A friend who wore one of Leading Lady's all-cotton bras swears by it, saying it made nursing so easy.

Nursing bras by Practical Elegance try to maintain the more feminine points of mainstream lingerie—and to a very large degree they succeed. Their lacy underwire nursing bra manages to be beautiful as well as functional.

The Nené bra was designed by Marguerite Williams to solve a number of problems. Its cup adjusts up three sizes, which means that the bra can often be worn from early on in pregnancy until the nursing

Wearing Bras to Bed?

Some women I talked to began wearing bras 24 hours a day as their pregnancies progressed. Is that really necessary? The experts I consulted felt that it was really a matter of personal comfort. If your breasts feel very heavy, you may enjoy the extra support of a bra. Will it prevent sagging? Gravity doesn't really come into play when you're lying down. One expert warned against wearing underwires to bed, because they may cut into your skin. Another suggested checking department stores for something called a leisure bra. This bra is made of stretch lace for soft, unstructured support.

period is over. The bra cup can remain on its larger hook immediately prior to nursing (when the breast is at its largest). After nursing, the cup can be adjusted down to accommodate the breasts' diminished size. Just like prenatal bras, the Nené has a four-hook adjustment in back. Sizes go from 34B to 38D.

Japanese Weekend now carries a bra in its O.K. line (see page 35). It is cotton, with lycra-faced cups, racer-style back, and a wrap front that provides extra support as well as nursing access.

The experts recommend purchasing nursing bras during your eighth month of pregnancy. At that point, your size is about the same as it will be after the baby is born. When they are first nursing, some women may get much bigger, but after the first week or two, most return to eighth-month size.

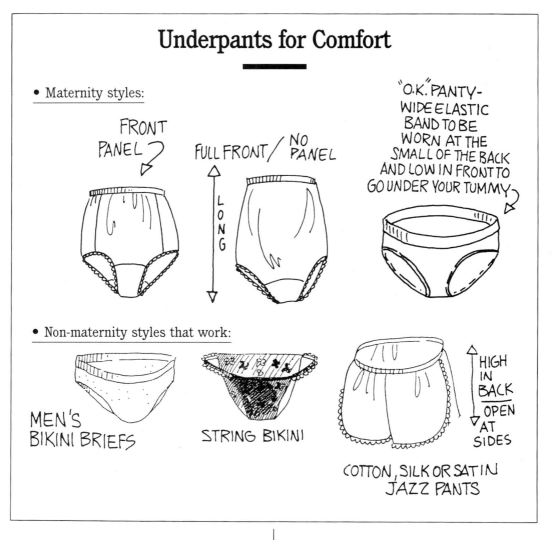

Underpants for Comfort

- Maternity styles:

FRONT PANEL

FULL FRONT / NO PANEL

LONG

"O.K." PANTY-WIDE ELASTIC BAND TO BE WORN AT THE SMALL OF THE BACK AND LOW IN FRONT TO GO UNDER YOUR TUMMY

- Non-maternity styles that work:

MEN'S BIKINI BRIEFS

STRING BIKINI

HIGH IN BACK OPEN AT SIDES

COTTON, SILK OR SATIN JAZZ PANTS

Do buy a minimum of two or three nursing bras. Leaking is common at the beginning, and you'll need to launder your bras often. Hormonal changes mean you'll be perspiring more. I found myself putting on a fresh bra every day and sometimes even more often. Go for the extra one or two. You'll be glad you have them.

Of course, there's no law that says you have to wear a special bra for nursing. One woman told me that when she wore a nursing bra, her bust looked like twin battleships had docked. Her solution was to buy regular stretch cotton underwire bras and either lift the cup over her breast to nurse or pull the cup down under her breast. She said it was great because she didn't have to unhook or unsnap anything. Another woman told me that she bought bras with center-front openings, which she just undid when she nursed. Someone else told me that she didn't bother with a nursing bra because she never felt comfortable nursing unless she took her top off and removed her entire bra. In the end it doesn't really matter which bra you use, just so long as you choose one that fits and supports you—and is easy to nurse in.

Underpants: The Real Bottom Line

In the course of my research, I found out that when it comes to underpants, pregnant women wear a surprisingly wide range of styles. They choose string or regular bikinis, hipsters, high-waisted briefs, all manner of maternity underpants, and even men's undies—from boxer shorts to bikinis. (I've already sung the praises of men's bikini underwear, without the pocket, in Chapter 1 and elsewhere.) Which choice is the correct one? That's easy. They all are. Where underpants are concerned, what's comfortable counts.

Do choose cotton for daily wear. It's more comfortable and absorbent. Save silky styles for special nights. As one woman put it, "When you're pregnant, you're so much warmer that cotton becomes a necessity."

Don't assume you can't be comfortable. Many of the women I talked to admitted that their underwear was either too tight or rolled down their tummies. One woman told me, "By the end, my underwear was so stretched out it practically fell down as I stood in the subway." Even if you can afford only two pairs of underwear that truly fit, buy them and do a wash every other night. It's well worth it. Executive Susan Fischer-Braun found that her bikini underwear wouldn't stay up after her seventh month. She switched to a maternity brief made by Hanro. Some women shy away from maternity underwear, repelled by their large look. But keep them in mind as you grow—they may be an oasis of comfort in the last months. Several styles are shown above right.

Look for comfortable details like wide stretch lace waist and leg openings. Barbara Cooke, of Joovay, a luxury lingerie shop in New York, reports that jazz pants are the new underpant of choice among pregnant women. Jazz pants have open-sided legs like some running shorts, which are very flattering, come comfortably up to the waist in the back, then dip lower—under the naval—in front. They come in cotton as well as in flashier silk or satin, and they're perfect for pregnancy and afterward.

The new O.K. panties by Japanese Weekend operate on the same under-the-tummy principle as their skirts and pants (see page 35). Their wide, soft elastic band offers a nice feeling of support.

Panty Hose

To get the widest range of styles and colors in panty hose, try regular queen sizes rather than maternity sizes. (If you need extra support because of a tendency toward varicose veins, see page 129.) Shop around to find brands with the most comfortable waistbands—wide and easy to stretch. Wear them over or tucked under your tummy, whichever is most comfortable. Susan Fischer-Braun found comfort in panty hose made by Ergee that had cotton rib-knit tops and stretchy, wide, nonbinding waistbands. Remember that matching hose to your skirt will lengthen your look. And if your legs are an asset, show them off in textured styles.

Slips

Even if you're not in the habit of wearing slips, you may come to appreciate the extra comfort they provide during pregnancy. If you wear bikini underwear, a slip can protect a sometimes sensitive belly from the layer of clothing on top. In the later months, your belly button may begin to protrude and can be irritated by fabrics that rub. A slip can smooth things over and camouflage the bump a bit. (A Band-Aid over your belly button may help, too!)

Third, a slip always helps fabric drape more fluidly over your body. This is a quality you will appreciate more and more as the months go by. There are lots of styles to choose from.

CAMISOLE

HALF SLIP
SLIT AT THE SIDE

MATERNITY SLIPS

You can choose to continue wearing your regular half-slip, pulling it up over your belly as you grow. If your whole slip is full enough, it may make it through the pregnancy. But you might want to switch to maternity slips at some point. Answers to my questionnaires were about equally divided between women who bought maternity slips and those who didn't. The advantage of a maternity slip is better fit—extra fullness is built in and hems are lower in front so they fall evenly over a protruding belly. What should help you decide is how you feel. It seems sensible to wear your old slips now, with the idea of wearing them out and purchasing some sexy new ones after the baby is born. But if you wear them and feel constricted, uncomfortable, and unattractive—is it really worth it? Go ahead and spring for a slip that fits. What's one little slip in the scheme of things?

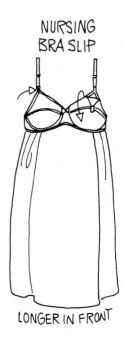

NURSING BRA SLIP

LONGER IN FRONT

HALF-SLIP OR WHOLE?

Some surveys have shown that most women continue wearing the kind of slip

HALF SLIP WITH FRONT PANEL CUT FOR FULLNESS

WHOLE SLIP

HEM IS LOWER IN FRONT

they wore before they got pregnant. But the questionnaires I received told a slightly different story. One woman began wearing a whole slip because "I felt that my pregnancy underwear was so ugly that I just felt prettier covering it all up with a pretty whole slip. Then when I walked around the bedroom in front of my husband while I was getting dressed, I didn't feel quite so self-conscious." That makes sense to me. Another woman switched to a whole slip when the elastic on her half-slip began to feel too binding and confining. She found that a whole nylon slip felt soft, silky, and smooth under her dresses.

A third option is to wear a camisole and a half-slip, both of which can be found in maternity styles. This is a nice option, giving you both coverage and versatility. The set I found was made in cotton and lace and was pretty enough to sleep in.

If you're pregnant in the summer months, do try to find slips in pure cotton. Cooler and more absorbent than blends, they're worth searching for. Most of the major manufacturers offer at least a few cotton styles. Just call the major maternity stores in your area to locate or order them.

Do you like bra slips? The Nené bra—that's the adjustable one that can be worn for both prenatal and nursing—comes with a slip attached. A nice way to streamline your lingerie.

Late at Night

Of course, no chapter about lingerie would be complete without talking about what you're going to wear to bed. When it's just the two of you, anything goes. You can be as lacy, luxurious, and all-out feminine as you please—pregnancy and all. You may have to pass on the teddies for now, but never mind. There's a whole world of generously cut and absolutely gorgeous nightgowns out there for you to splurge on. And, please, don't let a second of guilt cross your mind. These are purchases you won't pack away when your pregnancy's over.

Keep these cautions in mind when shopping for nightwear:

• Long gowns and robes will look more elegant and graceful than short. But make sure they're not so long that you're in danger of stumbling on the hems.

• Avoid designs that tie under the bust. They won't be as comfortable toward the end of your pregnancy. Choose gowns that flow from the shoulders.

• Remember that pregnancy makes you feel warmer. Cooler fabrics in short-sleeve or sleeveless styles may be most comfortable.

• Soft pastels like peach, pink, or blue are most flattering to unmade-up skin, according to Carole Hochman for Christian Dior.

A good support system is essential if you want to look and feel your best while you're pregnant. A little extra time and money spent on bras, underpants, panty hose, and slips that fit well will be repaid in comfort—a valuable commodity at this time in your life.

CHAPTER 10

D-Day and Beyond

Among the myriad answers I got to the question, "What clothes felt best during the last couple of months you were pregnant?" the most candid was: "What felt best was taking my clothes off!" Despite careful preparations, every woman experiences a sense of amazement at how big she eventually gets. "Huge is the word for what I got," magazine editor Janet Chan says. "The beauty of it was that I was so friendly with my belly I didn't care! As the months progressed, I felt an increased connection with the baby growing inside. When I ate, I imagined the food creating the baby's blood vessels and bones. It was like a high school science project. A complete marvel."

What to Wear in the Last Weeks

For the woman who works until delivery day or very close—and the number of women I talked to who went into labor at the office would make Gloria Steinem grin—the difference between the size she thinks she'll be and the size she actually becomes can create some last-minute sar-torial panic. "I learned my lesson the hard way," says one editor. "For months I got by with the bare minimum. I bought regular dresses at Loehmann's, wore some of my own dresses without the belts. Then, suddenly, in the last month and a half, they weren't big enough anymore. I was forced to break down and buy some bigger things. Since it was so close to the end, I didn't want to invest a lot of money. The funny thing is that if I'd had an inkling of just how expensive having a child was going to be, I wouldn't have made such a big deal about spending a little on some decent clothes. I would have felt better and looked better."

So what's the answer? Look back through the book for ideas on outfits that will stand the ultimate test—and stretch—of time. For me, a lifesaver was the kimono sewn up the front, shown on page 55. It was big, cool, and very cheap. In solid colors, worn with real jewelry like pearls and gold, kimonos can look conservative and appropriate enough for most offices. In splashy prints, they're perfect for casual dressing. Since it was midsummer, I usually tied the sleeves up with shoelaces or ribbon. I kept the hips sashed until the very end, when I didn't want the feeling of anything binding or close to the body. For cooler weather, you can choose satin instead of cotton, or warm up your kimono with a turtleneck sweater and tights.

The versatile elastic-topped dresses I've touted throughout the book, beginning in Chapter 2, are indispensable now. You'll welcome the feeling of freedom they allow, with just underpants and perhaps a half-slip underneath, but if you feel more comfortable wearing a bra, it's easy to add straps to the dress to hide your means of support. Dress up the look by throwing a shawl over one shoulder and securing it with a hip wrap, as shown. Or, if your wardrobe needs a lift, sew up a new dress for a few dollars. Choose a conservative fabric and you can probably wear it to the office with a jacket on top. If you're pining for a Laura Ashley dress but don't want to spend the money, buy Laura Ashley fabric instead and make an elastic-topped dress out of it. Add a petticoat underneath and you've got the look without the loss!

Another wonderful look for work late in the game is the coatdress shown on page 84, made from a man's antique paisley smoking jacket, with the belt loops removed and Velcro or buttons added for closure. Wear a whole slip underneath the coatdress to protect your privacy. You can find these jackets at thrift shops, and they're an even greater bargain because you can bring one to the hospital to wear as a robe. The jacket will make you feel very elegantly dressed as you walk down the hospital halls with your guests and linger outside the nursery, gazing at your sleeping baby. Since it opens in front, the jacket is perfect for nursing. And as you begin to lose weight, a belt will give it—and you—some shape. Using a leather belt, rather than the sash it comes with, will dress it up considerably. For all the wear you'll get out of this combination dress/

robe, you might want to invest in a new one—especially if your thrift shop hunts prove unsuccessful.

It might boost your spirits, as well as your wardrobe, to purchase a flowing dress you can use now—and later, by adding a belt. Judging from the women I polled, Laura Ashley is doing a booming business with future moms because they offer just such styles in their regular line. Even women who'd never thought of wearing the small-print, ruffly, or lacy dresses before found themselves gravitating toward them by the end of their pregnancies. "They made me feel feminine when all I felt was big and clumsy. By the ninth month, I craved ruffles!" said one new mom. "They were big and comfortable and

THE VERSATILE DRESS IS PERFECT NOW

ANTIQUE SHAWL

OVERLAP POINTS OF SHAWL AND SECURE WITH A HIP WRAP

Wrap a shawl across to dress it up.

crisp—and because they were all cotton they were cool, too," said another. These dresses also come in corduroys and wool blends for winter.

Alot of women had invested in Laura Ashley or other voluminous dresses with the idea of wearing them later, but I wondered how many actually did. For the most part, women who felt comfortable in—and not overwhelmed by—bigger clothes *did* continue to wear and enjoy them. This was true especially if they liked the style of the dresses to begin with. And they were a godsend for women who lost their weight slowly. "By the time my maternity leave was up, I still hadn't lost all my weight, and I couldn't get back into my regular clothes. Thank goodness I had a few big dresses I could belt. They got me through!" one woman told me.

Magazine editor Judsen Culbreth felt that dresses in heavier fabrics like gabardine gave a crisper, more professional appearance in the last months. "They held their shape and therefore looked better."

As my pregnancy came to an end, I found myself doing more and more wrapping of fabric. The bathing suit made out of a pareo and bikini pants (see Chapter 6) was super comfortable to wear around the house, with another pareo wrapped at the hips as a skirt. Caftans shortened to just below the knees, worn with the sleeves rolled, were another favorite. They're light, cool, comfortable, and usually done in soft fabrics that drape beautifully.

Marie Louise Marco, ex-model and director of Fam Model Management in Paris, was in her ninth month during the winter, and she wore her husband's overalls and sweatshirts almost exclusively. They could be washed and worn over and over, getting softer and more cozy each time. Many of the menswear ideas I've discussed throughout the book come in especially handy now.

The bottom line at this stage is comfort. You're at your largest, you're getting anxious about the big event, and you need ease and comfort. By now you should be expert enough at fashion brainstorming to tackle this final challenge.

Organization with a Capital "O"

The most important thing to do in the ninth month is *get organized.* I was calm as could be before my first was born . . . and in a complete panic afterward. With my second, I was ready. Before your baby is born, it's impossible to imagine how different life will become in a few short weeks. Suddenly, it's not so easy to go back to a store if you forgot something. As a matter of fact, it's not so easy to get to a store in the first place. And you're so busy! Women who work think they know what busy is. It's *nothing* compared to having a child. For one thing, workdays end. Baby care goes on 24 hours a day. One friend told me that she imagined her maternity leave as an idyllic period of rest, relaxation, and peaceful communing with her newborn. A colicky baby that woke up three or four times a night burst that bubble fast. That's not to say caring for your newborn isn't wonderful. It is, of course. It's just a more *exhausting* wonderful than you might expect.

PLAN NOW FOR LATER

One of the best moves you can make is to plan for your postnatal wardrobe several months in advance of your due date. I remember seeing a photograph of one well-known model two weeks after her son was born, wearing the kind of body-hugging gown that most women couldn't get away with under normal conditions. But that, alas, is not the norm. Most of us take a good two months, and often more, before we fit comfortably back into our regular clothes.

A corporate executive had her first baby at the end of spring. By the time she got out of the hospital it was summer and there was a heat wave to boot. With the 20 extra pounds she was still carrying, there was no way she was going to put on shorts or "anything else I owned." What she did do was to duck into the first store she could get to and buy up all the loose jumpsuits and drawstring pants she could find. "I felt better about the way I looked, but not about spending that sizable chunk of money. I really felt backed up against the wall clothes-wise."

A better idea is to take advantage of the relative freedom you have before the baby is born. If you do decide to purchase a few new things, you won't feel as pressured into buying them quickly as you might later, when you have little time and a baby-sitter to pay in order to shop. Before the baby is born, you can take the time to really look around and analyze what you need.

A good postnatal wardrobe should consist of clothes you can launder easily. The facts of life are that new moms leak and stain and new babies spit up and wet through their diapers. It's not pretty, but there it is. That's why a generous supply of T-shirts, sweatshirts, sweatpants, and pareos is so essential. I'll never forget the story a friend told me about how she brought home an outfit from a store to try on. While she had it on, and she and her husband were discussing whether or not to keep it, her two-week-old baby decided he was ready to nurse. She sat down and proceeded to feed him. As she switched the baby from one breast to the other, she noticed a yellow stain spreading on the lap of her not-yet-decided-upon pants. Decision made!

Should you plan to wear maternity clothes postmaternity? That's the plan a lot of women had—until the time came to actually put it into action. It seems reasonable enough, but somehow it just goes against human nature to continue wearing maternity clothing after the baby has been delivered. As one woman said, "There I was pushing the baby carriage and wearing a maternity dress and it just felt all wrong. It sounds funny, but I felt as

POSTNATAL SUMMER ESSENTIALS

Substitute sweatsuits in winter.

An antique cotton nightshirt is cool and comfortable right through the last weeks. Sash it under your tummy or let it flow.

though I didn't deserve to wear maternity clothes anymore." Of course, you should wear whatever is comfortable, but it's wise not to count too much on continuing with maternity wear.

If you've been wearing the non-maternity alternatives I've suggested—including clothes one size larger than usual, or with more fabric than the styles you'd usually choose—you won't have to make this maternity-wear-after-birth decision. Simply plan to adapt what you've been wearing to your postnatal body with belts and sashes. Go back and take a look at the clothes you wore in the third, fourth, and fifth months of your pregnancy. The way your body looked then will probably be close to its shape after giving birth. If the season is very different, you'll have to improvise accordingly. I went back to the men's pants, suspenders, and shirts I'd been wearing until about the eighth month. Instead of wearing the men's suits I had worn a lot, though, I stuck to cotton khakis and other casual pants. Because they were roomy, they didn't put pressure on the sensitive area around my episiotomy. As my waist shrank, I added a necktie as a belt for fun and variety. I continued to wear my pareos and elastic-topped dresses. Both were perfect for nursing.

Whatever you choose, expect to wear twice as many clothes as you would normally. If you have a washer and dryer handy, this may not be a problem. If you don't, you may want to consider having more clothes on hand. It's sheer numbers that are important here because the point is to feel clean and fresh. At the beginning, even that is a challenge. Stylist Marilise Flusser remembers how crazy things got. "My mother said that all I did when I visited her was wash and blow-dry my hair and take pictures! With my second baby, I couldn't even manage that much!" I recommend buying several packages of men's T-shirts and boxer shorts if it's summer, sweatsuits if it's winter. You don't have to go public with the boxer shorts, but for hanging around the house, they're perfect. Consider pareos, too—or simply lengths of cotton fabric twice your hip measurement tied on as skirts. They're cheap, easy to wash, and nice to walk around in, as well as being cool, feminine, and pretty.

If you haven't already, buy a comfortable pair of flat, slip-on shoes. Believe it or not, you'll appreciate saving even the few seconds it takes to tie laces—which you can't do with a baby in your arms, anyway.

STOCK UP ON SUPPLIES

Having a baby is like inviting a hurricane to come and stay. Permanently. However, unlike a hurricane, a baby makes you feel that even though your life will never be the same, you wouldn't have it any other way. Still, it's a good idea to batten down the hatches, stock up on supplies, and take care of business well in advance of his or her arrival. Here are some things to collect in the calm before the storm.

For yourself:

• Buy a six-month supply of your most-used beauty products.

• Assemble a box of barrettes, clips, elastic bands, scarves, mousse, and gel so you won't be caught short.

• At least two weeks before your due date, get your hair trimmed and have a facial. You just won't have the time or inclination afterward. Why two weeks? One friend who made her facial appointment for a week in advance of her due date had a week-old baby at that point.

• Get manicures and pedicures as needed. As you get closer to your date, consider choosing paler nail colors or just clear gloss. You probably won't have time for regular manicures after the baby is born, and paler colors show chips less than darker ones do.

• Respect your condition. When you're tired, slow down. Put your feet up. Relax. Get regular sleep, difficult as it may become toward the end.

• Invest in a hand massager to soothe sore muscles and feet.

For the house:

• Buy or borrow an answering machine, if you don't already have one. Congratulatory phone calls are wonderful, but they can interrupt much-needed sleep. Before you nap, or when you're with your baby, shut the phones off and turn the machine on. Return the calls when it's convenient for you.

• Gather together all your best, quickest recipes. For a while, preparing even the simplest dinner will seem like a major intrusion. Simple, easy, reliable recipes can take the planning part out of it.

• Stock up on your family's favorite frozen foods. If friends ask if they can do anything, ask them to cook and freeze a meal.

• Pay bills, insurance, taxes, as far ahead as you can.

• Write all important dates and birthdays on your calendar for the next six months. Having a baby tends to blot out everything else that's going on. But you'll feel better if you don't lose sight of everything completely. Fill out birthday cards and envelopes as far in advance as you think is reasonable. Write the "to send" date in the upper right corner where the stamp will cover it. If Mother's or Father's Day is coming up, have gifts ready to be given or sent.

• Make a list of phone numbers for the best take-out places—especially those that deliver—and tape it to the refrigerator. If you have a supermarket and pharmacy with delivery services, note those, too.

• Keep your car's gas tank full!

• Store any items needing extra care that you won't have time to give: silver, knick-knacks that need a lot of dusting, and the like.

• Stock up on light bulbs, soap, toothpaste, deodorant, paper goods, laundry detergent for family and baby, soft drinks and juices, garbage bags for the baby's diaper pail, diaper-pail deodorizers—and diapers.

• Take care of all house and car maintenance.

• Put away all your fresh-flower vases and replace them with maintenance-free dried or silk flower arrangements.

• Purchase your layette, including a going-home outfit for the baby and a few things in sizes 6 to 12 months—babies grow fast!

• Hire a housecleaner or housecleaning service to come in and help you as often as your budget allows.

• Address and stamp birth announcements. If you're having them printed, ask the printer to give you the envelopes now.

• Buy loads of film and make sure your camera is in good repair.

Packing Your Hospital Bag

"My friends keep asking me if I have my bag packed yet," said one mother I talked to, who was eight months pregnant at the time. "It's funny, but I have put it off. Keeping a packed suitcase sitting in my bedroom ready to go makes it seem even more real! I'm not sure I'm ready yet."

While first-time mothers usually delay packing, most second-time mothers make sure they have their bags organized and ready to go well ahead of time. "When my first baby was born I took a really casual attitude toward what I brought. Then when the time came, I found myself wishing I had packed a lot more carefully," one friend told me. Another mother of two said, "The time after the baby is born is so confusing, overwhelming, and joyous and painful all wrapped into one that even a seemingly small thing like having what you need and want where you need it can be a comfort in itself." The lesson seems to be, again, to plan ahead. Here are the necessities—as well as the treats—that many women were glad to have along.

A couple of spirit-lifting nightgowns and a really special bathrobe come first, because most of the women I talked to felt strongly about them. Many wore the hospital's nightgowns for the first few days so that they didn't stain their own with the discharge that follows birth. But they were happy to have something nice to change into during visiting hours. One woman continued to wear hospital gowns but hid them under a fancy paisley robe (see page 84).

Marilise Flusser splurged on a new crisp nightgown and robe at Laura Ashley and bought hair ribbons to match. A saleswoman commented, "I found it very strange to wear nightgowns all day long, so I brought a robe that looked more like an at-home dress than sleepwear. It made me feel more dressed." Patricia Davant, a dancer, brought a men's pajama top in white with blue piping. "It was perfect for nursing—easy to open or lift up—and didn't get all wrapped and bunched up around my legs the way nightgowns do."

The perfect gown for the hospital, according to Barbara Cooke, of Joovay lingerie shop, is calf-length or shorter. You want to avoid a gown that is so long it could trip you up while carrying the baby. She advises selecting a comfortable, soft cotton. For some time after delivery, the change in

From the Mouths of Baby Nurses

If anybody knows what a newborn needs, it's a baby nurse. After all, dealing with newborns is her stock in trade. Here, then, is the quintessential baby nurse's list of indispensables for new moms:

- unscented baby wipes
- diapers—disposable and cotton
- baby bath soap
- baby lotion
- cornstarch
- sterile cotton balls and pads (size 3 x 3)
- diaper-rash cream
- tubes of petroleum jelly
- fabric softener
- gentle laundry detergent
- wool wash, in winter
- baby nail scissors
- antibiotic ointment
- alcohol
- cotton swabs
- washcloths and soft towels
- paper towels

hormones may result in night sweats, and silky fabrics are not as absorbent or cool as cotton. (Of course, they're fine for dressing up during visiting hours.) Look for styles you'll feel comfortable wearing to walk down the hospital halls and receive visitors. If you plan to breastfeed, look for gowns with button fronts. Eileen West for Queen Anne's Lace makes beautifully feminine ones. Practical Elegance makes stylish cotton gowns especially for nursing. Avoid open lace and lots of ribbons, which babies love to get their fingers tangled up in. And go for pockets for extra convenience.

Next, make it easy on yourself and get a pair of slip-on slippers, so you don't have to bend down to put them on. And opt for low heels. College professor Diana Martland picked out a pair of high-heeled mules for the hospital, fantasizing that they'd be just the thing to lift her spirits. What actually happened was that she was in so much pain that when the time came to step into the slippers, she couldn't even maintain her balance. "But they did look awfully pretty standing by my bed!" she maintains. With her second baby, it was flats all the way!

As I mentioned in the last chapter, nursing bras are best bought in the eighth month to get the right size. You should have at least two bras so you can wash one out in the hospital sink while you're wearing the other. Don't forget nursing pads, available in most drugstores. These are little blotters designed to be placed right over your nipples to soak up leaking milk. One new mom told me, "Until I discovered nursing pads, I had to change my bras and tops constantly. Those little pads helped me keep my sanity!" If you don't plan to nurse, pack two snug-fitting bras—just about any of your regular bras will fill this bill—and you can use pads in these, as well.

Some women advise wearing your maternity underwear in the hospital so that if it gets stained you can just throw it out. Others say that fresh, new cotton underwear feels better. If you do buy new underwear, make it white for easier bleaching and buy it at least one size larger than your prepregnancy size. Said one new mom, "Waist-high underpants from the five-and-dime store felt great after my C-section. There was no elastic near the stitches."

The hospital will provide sanitary napkins—special, extra-big, heavy-duty ones. Nowadays many of the napkins are self-adhesive, but bring along two sanitary belts just in case. Some women find regular napkins more comfortable and just as effective. You might pack some so you'll have an option.

BRING SOME FAVORITE THINGS WITH YOU TO THE HOSPITAL

Of course you'll need two going-home outfits—one for you and one for the baby. Stay away from baby gowns with drawstring bottoms. These don't allow you to fasten the car-seat strap between his or her legs for the trip home. Other items you'll appreciate having along include a radio, a cassette recorder, a notebook for recording

A Surprising Solution for a Common Problem

Having your water break at home and then getting to the hospital with water puddling around your legs is an uncomfortable, not to mention embarrassing, situation. Here's a better idea, from a New York obstetrician: Pick up—well ahead of time—a couple of packages of adult diapers. You can get them at any surgical supply store, as well as in many drugstores. Put one on when your water breaks, letting it ride under your tummy, and wear it to the hospital.

One friend who had to take a taxi to the hospital was incredibly relieved to have followed this advice. She even continued to wear the diapers for a few days after her baby was born. She found them much more comfortable than sanitary belts and pads, and they made her feel cleaner and fresher. It's a good way, too, to avoid ruining or staining underwear.

thoughts and feelings, and books and magazines. You might bring one of the books on baby care you didn't have time to read before the big event. There's nothing like having a baby in your arms to ignite the flame of learning! Don't forget such necessities as glasses and/or contact lens solution and storage case, and cosmetics and toiletries (you'll find more on these on page 151).

To Pack Separately—Your Childbirth Bag

If you are planning to have natural childbirth, what you pack for comfort during labor is just as important as what you take for your stay in the hospital. Make up a small, separate bag for these lifesavers:

- The items specified by your prepared-childbirth instructor. (These vary from class to class.)

- Some quick refreshers, like Vaseline, to keep your lips from cracking, and breath spray, less for use as a breath-freshener than to give you a better taste in your mouth. One actress's husband had the wonderful idea of packing an herbal water spray from a health-food store to refresh her with during labor.

- Snacks for your husband. Energizers like nuts and raisins or protein bars, and mouth fresheners like gum and mints.

- Camera, film, and flashbulbs.

Bring along your phone book and a roll of quarters. One woman I know copied all the numbers she wanted to call right after the baby was born onto a separate sheet of paper so she wouldn't have to thumb through her book and wouldn't risk missing anyone important in the chaos that followed the birth.

Finally, fill the nooks and crannies of your suitcase with a few mementos from home. It's amazing what an emotional lift you can get from seeing a favorite photo or knickknack in an otherwise impersonal hospital room. One secretary recalled, "It was really cold in my room, so I asked my husband to bring a quilt from home. I loved having it there. I had also packed some pictures of my husband, which I kept on my bedside table." A beautifully scented sachet will also help your room seem more homey.

Remember to Soothe the Siblings

If this isn't your first child, you need to be aware of how the sibling(s)-to-be will feel about your absence, and your return with a new family member. Spend some time planning how to ease their anxieties and include them in the joy.

It must be acknowledged that material objects carry some weight at this time. (Of course, they are always backed by love.) So, buy small gifts for your other child or children and tuck them into your hospital bag. The first thing my son, then five, said to me on seeing his new sister surrounded with gifts was, "Where's mine?" I was able to pull out a surprise that made him feel included. Data processor Pat Martland had another idea. She knew exactly what to expect by the time her fourth child was born—and she was prepared. "Before I left for the hospital, I hid gifts all over the house, one for each child, for each day I was going to be away. Then, when I talked to them from the hospital, I told them where to look for their special presents. When I came home with the baby, I also had prepared a gift for each child from the baby. It really seemed to soothe ruffled feathers." When friends call and ask if you need anything, suggest small gifts for the siblings.

Try to spend even more time with your child before the new baby comes. Pick up some of the very good books around that describe what's going to happen and help the child deal with the event and his or her feelings. For suggestions, ask at your local library or children's bookstore. If your due date is near any holidays or birthdays, prepare for them ahead of time. Plan a party for a birthday, buy Christmas or Hanukkah presents, or get Easter baskets ready.

Make plans that will keep the child's world as stable as possible. Be sure he or she has enough clothes and shoes in the right sizes for several months ahead. Give thought to nursery school or other school arrangements, if necessary, so you don't have to panic about that later.

The Double Hospital Gown

———

One solution to a drafty and revealing hospital gown is to ask for two. Put one on back-to-front and the second on front-to-back, as shown.

The Beauty Part— Cosmetics and Toiletries to Pack

You may think that your looks are the last thing you're going to worry about in the hospital, but you'd be surprised. A birth is a long-prepared-for event. Like a wedding, the birth of a baby marks a passage, a moment we've pictured in our minds for years. When it finally arrives, the role of the glowing, beautiful mother is one we have a strong impulse to play. Said one new mom, "I felt so vain, but I have to admit the thought occurred to me nonetheless. The pictures being taken at the hospital will become the history of my family. When my husband and new son look through the album in the years to come, I want them to remember me with my hair in place and my cheeks rosy!"

Susan Fischer-Braun had a fantasy of how she would look with her newborn baby. She would be sitting up in bed, both she and the baby dressed in white. And with her lace nightgown and her baby's white knit outfit, that's exactly how it was.

Here are suggestions from some new moms on how to stock your hospital makeup bag. Pick and choose among them according to your own preferences.

• Your regular makeup packed in a small cosmetics bag

• A good-smelling new shampoo

• A special soap. Crabtree & Evelyn and Henri Bendel's soaps were top choices.

• Toothbrush and toothpaste

• Brush and comb

• Tissues

• Razor

• Deodorant

• Hairstyling equipment

• Shower cap

• Scented body lotion

• Manicure kit, or at least a nail file and clippers

• Dusting power to absorb perspiration and keep skin from feeling sticky during postnatal heat flashes

• Skin freshener and cotton balls. One woman reported, "I applied it constantly at the beginning because I was so warm. It made me feel cool, fresh, clean."

Coming Home

The passage into motherhood presents a challenge for even the most prepared, best-organized women. At the beginning, there's always something unexpected, something new to deal with, some situation you hadn't planned for. Experienced mothers just laugh and say it's good training for the years ahead. The important thing is to create realistic expectations for yourself. Things may not be perfect, but then again, that's perfectly all right.

Remember, for every mother who is blissful from day one, there's another mother who feels guilty because she isn't. "When I had my first baby, I went immediately into panic mode," remembers Eva Cooperman, a language arts consultant. "I didn't know what to do with him. I didn't know how to take care of him. I didn't know how to nurse him. I didn't know how to put him to sleep or stop him crying. And, of course, I thought I was the only one who felt that way." Ex-Joffrey Ballet dancer and physical therapist Mara Abrams concurs: "I was in total shock. Nursing was uncomfortable. I was uncomfortable. I don't think I slept a wink for three weeks." Architect Alicia Emery loved being pregnant but was totally in the dark about what would happen after the baby was born. "I assumed that we'd go home,

New Hairdos for Hospital and After

No matter how practical you consider your haircut to be, motherhood can teach you otherwise. Here are some quick, pretty, new-mom hairdos you can master in a flash.

- French braids are pretty and practical. Practice them now, before the baby is born, so you can do them easily later.

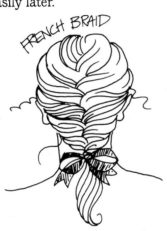

- Make a modified French braid with elastics, as shown.

- Add volume and style to short, wavy hair with a dollop of mousse. Scrunch hair in your fingers as you blow it dry.

- Tie long hair back with elastic and cover with a pretty scarf or ribbon.

- Make a romantic braid by bending over, braiding hair, and then standing up. The result will be a full, soft frame for your face.

- Do two braids Pocahontas-style and pin them up on top of your head.

- If you have medium-length hair, twist the sides back and secure them with barrettes.

- When all else fails and you have to appear in public, resort to my two-second disaster look. Put on a hat, a really interesting pair of sunglasses, and a great-color lipstick.

Defensive Dressing

—————

Babies have a charming way of wreaking havoc on even the most baby-proofed outfits. But there are safeguards. Take some tips from the experts—a few new moms I know:

- Learn the art of camouflage. A cluster of pins can hide a stain near a collar. A scarf, strategically placed, can hide even more. A huge square shawl or even a sweatshirt can be wrapped around your waist or hips to hide an accident when a change of clothes isn't handy.

- Become a fan of the layered look: Add a shirt or sweatshirt on top of a soiled garment. A jacket over a shirt. You get the idea.

- Keep plenty of extra T-shirts, boxers, sweatsuits, and pareos around for quick changes.

- Buy some cloth diapers—for yourself! Part of a new mom's uniform is a diaper on the shoulder, for wiping baby's face and protecting your own clothes.

"I felt really betrayed," says attorney Madeline Kuflik. "According to my childbirth classes, delivery was bliss and nothing afterward was ever even discussed. The fact is that delivery is the most painful experience in the world, and afterward you're a mess. You're exhausted, in pain, totally confused, you know nothing about taking care of a baby, and neither does your husband. I think it's awful that *someone* doesn't prepare you for the aftermath."

One of the best moves a new mother can make to ease these problems is to connect with a support group. This can be a formal group, meeting at a Y or childhood education center, or it can spring up spontaneously through informal networks—childbirth-class friends who all have babies the same age, or parents of playmates at the local park. Alicia Emery credits her group with saving her sanity in the beginning. "We shared our problems and concerns. Just hearing that what your baby is going through appears to be normal can be so comforting when everything is new and such a mystery."

If you're very lucky, you have a family who want to do everything they can for you. The time following the birth of a baby is very special not only for you, but for your parents. Chances are your parents and friends will be respectful of your need to recuperate. If they aren't, it's up to you to tell them you need rest. Limit the number of people you see and the length of time they stay. Practice saying, "Doctor's orders." It is, in fact, true. Any doctor will tell you that rest will speed your recovery.

Expect—but don't be upset by—any criticism you may receive on caring for your baby. When it comes to baby care, everyone considers him- or herself an expert. Simply smile and let it pass. You are the baby's mother—what you say goes!

go to sleep, and wake up the next morning all at the same time. The reality was that my baby slept during the day and was awake all night. After three days of this I was in a total frenzy! I remember calling up my uncle and asking him when I was going to be able to get some rest. His answer? 'Oh, in about twenty years, sweetie.' He wasn't too far off!"

One-Handed Makeup—and Some Postpartum Tips

There exists a baby who will sit contentedly while you do your makeup and comb your hair. I don't know of one myself, but I'm told he or she exists. For the rest of us, there is the following technique. I learned it as a model, but I use it more than ever as a mother. It allows you to put on makeup with one hand, while you bounce a fussy baby with the other.

You will need: an artist's palette, or any old tray, plus your favorite makeup (covers removed), a strong glue, and an orange-juice can.

The strategy is to glue the makeup containers to the tray so that they can't move around as you dip into them with your free hand. I put my eye makeup next to my blush, next to a pot of lip color. Mascara can be glued on in a stand-up position. The caps of eye and lip pencils can be glued on so the pencils can then slide easily into place. Glue on the orange-juice can to hold brushes and combs.

Keep the tray on your dresser or sink, ready for use.

Even with this trouble-saver, you won't often have time to do a full makeup job. All you really need to look and feel attractive is a touch-up that takes your condition and schedule into account. Try this:

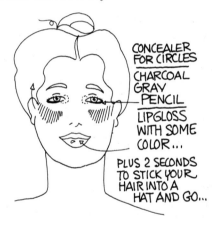

CONCEALER FOR CIRCLES
CHARCOAL GRAY PENCIL
LIPGLOSS WITH SOME COLOR...
PLUS 2 SECONDS TO STICK YOUR HAIR INTO A HAT AND GO...

- Blend some concealer under and at inside corners of your eyes to hide circles caused by interrupted sleep.

- Apply a natural-looking pink or peach blush to cheekbones, blending it into your hairline to minimize puffiness.

- Dash on some gray pencil at outside corners and lower lids, smudging with your finger for a soft line.

- Dab on some lightly colored lip gloss, tie up your hair, and go!

COMBS AND LONG MAKE-UP BRUSHES
SMALL JUICE CAN
CAKE MASCARA
LIP GLOSS
EYE SHADOW
GLUE LOW BOX FOR SMALL BRUSHES
POWDER BLUSH
CAKE LINER

GLUE YOUR MAKEUP ESSENTIALS ONTO AN ARTISTS PALLETTE

BABY YOURSELF

Remember when your mother used to say, "Never do two things at once"? Well, forget about that now, because the only way you're going to have any time for yourself is to learn the art of doubling up. For example, when you first begin nursing, you'll want to revel in the bond between baby and yourself. But after a few weeks you may realize that this is a time you can use to catch up on the world at large. You'll find that while you're nursing you can read the newspaper, watch a news show, return phone calls, or listen to music. When the baby's napping (another short time-out), take a quick shower, put on fresh clothes, and relax! Or take the time to prepare everything for when he or she wakes up. Work out a schedule with your husband in which you share duties after he gets home.

Of course, if you can afford extra help, employ a qualified nurse or housekeeper. Keep lists of things you want to do, so that when you do have a moment you'll know exactly what they were. A kind of senility settles in after giving birth!

A New Life

You and I are very lucky. Lucky to have had our babies in these times of practically limitless possibilities. Lucky to have had the pluck to express ourselves as we like—in our clothing as well as in other areas of our lives. Lucky to have had the health and energy and vitality to get through it all.

Congratulations. You did it. You're a family! And the best is yet to come. I wish you all good luck!